The Allegany Senecas and Kinzua Dam

The Allegany Senecas

and Kinzua Dam

Forced Relocation through

Two Generations

JOY A. BILHARZ

University of Nebraska Press

Lincoln and London

© 1998 by the University
of Nebraska Press
All rights reserved
Manufactured in the United States
of America
The paper in this book
meets the minimum requirements
of American National Standard
for Information Sciences—Permanence
of Paper for Printed Library
Materials, ANSI Z39.48-1984.
Library of Congress
Cataloging-in-Publication Data
Bilharz, Joy Ann.
The Allegany Senecas and Kinzua
Dam: forced relocation through
two generations / Joy A. Bilharz.
    p. cm.
Includes bibliographical
reference (p.) and index.
ISBN 0-8032-1282-8 (Cl.: alk. paper)
1. Seneca Indians—Relocation.
2. Indian land transfers—
New York (State)
3. Dams—New York (State)
I. Title.
E99.S3B45   1998
974.7'0049755–dc21
97-35056
CIP

*To the memory of
Joseph H. Bilharz and
Cornelius Abrams Jr.*

Contents

Illustrations

MAPS

Acknowledgments

This book would not have been possible without the cooperation, support, and encouragement of the people of the Allegany Reservation of the Seneca Nation of Indians. They welcomed me into their homes and shared painful reminiscences, family albums, good food, raucous softball games, and quiet peaceful walks along the river. Many of the people with whom I worked closely have died since I first went to Allegany. As Claire Farrer has noted (1996, 10), it is often hard to return to a place knowing familiar faces will no longer be there to greet you. Long-term fieldwork entails times of great sadness as well as happiness.

There are too many Senecas who helped me to thank each individually; only one person refused to talk with me about the removal, because, in her words, "They wouldn't let you write what I think." I hope in some small way I have been able to document the grief and anguish behind her decision. To all of the Allegany people, a heartfelt *nyah:weh!*

I would, however, like to acknowledge the deep debt I owe to Du-Wayne "Duce," Janis, Pam, Michelle, and Guy Bowen, who always made me feel welcome in their home. Midge Dean Stock, Becki Bowen, Carol Moses, Elmer John, George and David Heron, Walter Taylor, Jeff Snow, Lehman "Dar" Dowdy, Bob Hoag, Sandy Jimerson, Richard, Leitha, Kevin, and Mike Johnny-John, and Nettie Watt all shared their reflections with me on many occasions and taught me much about life at Allegany. Harriett Pierce and Inez Redeye kept me laughing and learning through many rainy days spent in the library. The staff at Highbanks Campground and the Allegany Branch of the Seneca Nation Library were unfailingly kind and helpful.

The fieldwork portion of this research was funded by Grant #4718 from the Wenner-Gren Foundation for Anthropological Research. Additional archival research was supported by a Scholarly Incentive Grant from the State University of New York College at Fredonia.

Versions of this manuscript have been read and critiqued by Cornelius Abrams Jr., Duce Bowen, Harriett Pierce, and Inez Redeye. It is far better because of their insight. I am also grateful for comments and suggestions from Drs. Thomas Abler, Thayer Scudder, Deborah Welch, William Fenton, Anthony F. C. Wallace, Jane Goodale, and Laurence Hauptman, although I am solely responsible for the final product. The Annual Conference on Iroquois Research was a useful sounding board as the work evolved. Mary Castor-Rudolph provided constant support and a home away from home in which to write. Jane Curran's thoughtful contributions and editorial skills have helped throughout the editing process.

My friends and colleagues in the Department of Sociology and Anthropology provided encouragement in many ways. Alan La-Flamme cheerfully read each revision and made lots of dinners. Peter Sinden developed nagging into an art form that ensured that the work was finally brought to a conclusion. Richard Reddy provided invaluable help on the fine points of computers and word processing whenever I encountered problems. Joyce Stephens made sure I took a break every Thursday afternoon. Lee Braude and William Muller (Department of Political Science) kept me laughing through the final preparation and provided helpful comments. The staff of Reed Library at SUNY Fredonia, especially Janet Ferry and Marianne Eimer of the Interlibrary Loan Department, were unfailingly helpful.

My daughter, Nancy, shared the better part of two summers living in a tent with me at Highbanks. Her running commentary on events helped temper my forays into cynicism and elation, and in her willingness to review field notes she often reminded me of data I had forgotten and provided interesting and useful perspectives. Sharing the fieldwork experience with her made it less stressful, and I am grateful for her companionship.

This book is dedicated to the memory of my father, Joseph H. Bilharz, from whom I first learned of the injustices done to the Allegany Senecas and who died only weeks before the book went to press. In his ninety-eighth year he was still able to vividly recall the events of the decade of removal. He was a kind and gentle man who always believed the best about people and government and was deeply troubled when that trust was betrayed. This dedication also serves to recognize the contributions of the many non-Indians who supported the Seneca Nation.

This book also is dedicated to the memory of Cornelius Abrams Jr., former councilor and director of the Maps and Boundary Department for the Seneca Nation, a man whose vision for the Seneca Nation was never realized because of his premature death. Corny was a walking archive whose wisdom, knowledge, and friendship are sorely missed by those of us fortunate enough to have known him.

Introduction: Learning from the Senecas

Between 1959 and 1964, the U.S. Army Corps of Engineers undertook the construction of a 179-foot dam on the Allegheny River in Warren, Pennsylvania (see map 1). Its reservoir, with a maximum capacity of 21,188 acres, flooded one-third of the Allegany Reservation of the Seneca Nation of Indians in western New York, leaving untouched only wooded hillsides and towns occupied by whites under leases executed by Congress in the late nineteenth century (see map 2). The construction of Kinzua Dam resulted in the relocation of 550 Seneca people, which William Fenton (1967, 7) has called "one of the most interesting social experiments of our time . . . an experiment in directed culture change."

The objective of this study is to trace over thirty years the reaction of the Senecas to their relocation. The case study is placed within a comparative framework using a model of long-term response to resettlement developed by Thayer Scudder and Elizabeth Colson based on their study of the Kariba Dam in Zambia. The Allegany Reservation provided an ideal situation for this. There were extensive historical records generated by Senecas and non-Senecas, and many of the people most directly involved still lived on or near the reservation and were able to provide their own insights and recollections. Information on pre-dam conditions was gathered from reservation newsletters, local papers and archives, Seneca Nation documents, a pre-relocation survey done by the Bureau of Indian

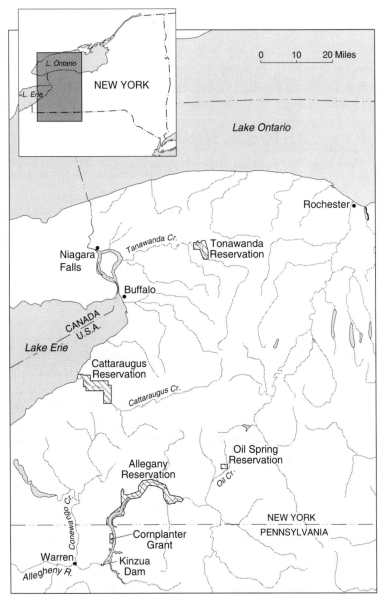

1. Seneca Lands in New York and Pennsylvania (after Abler and Tooker 1978). The Cattaraugus, Oil Spring, and Allegany Reservations belong to the Seneca Nation of Indians. The Tonawanda Reservation belongs to the Tonawanda Band of Senecas.

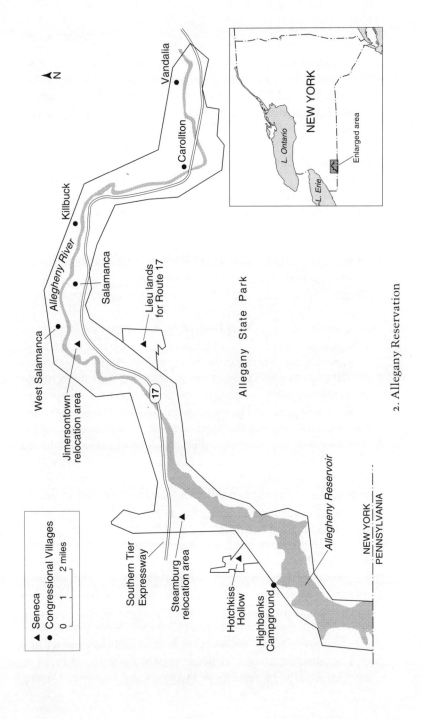

2. Allegany Reservation

Affairs (Fuhriman 1963), and reminiscences of residents. Post-relocation studies conducted by anthropology students (Feldsher 1970; Feldsher and Williams 1972) provided data on the years immediately following removal. In addition, there is considerable documentation of Iroquois political activities on the state and federal levels (Hauptman 1981, 1986a, 1986b, 1988; Vecsey and Starna 1988; Campisi 1984), which is useful in placing the Seneca struggle within a broader political context. Because the Nation's enrollment records are closed to outsiders, it was not possible to compare Allegany residents who were forced to relocate with those who were not since there was no way to compile a list of the latter individuals. The number of people who lost neither their homes nor significant portions of their land was so small that a comparison, while interesting, would probably not be significant.

Permission to undertake field research at Allegany was granted in May 1985 by Lionel John, treasurer of the Seneca Nation of Indians (SNI) and highest elected official on the Allegany Reservation. The Seneca president, Calvin Lay, assured me that since my work would involve only people on the Allegany Reservation, I could proceed without the permission of the SNI Council, provided John approved. Subsequently I met with several Allegany councilors as well as the treasurer, and the permission was confirmed in writing. A complicating factor at this time was the increase in political activism on the reservation, culminating in a nationally publicized attempt to halt construction of the Southern Tier Expressway (New York Route 17) through the reservation. All outsiders were closely scrutinized, as rumors of an influx of agitators were common. Despite the increased tension, members of both factions accepted my presence on the reservation.

My initial goal upon moving to the reservation in the summer of 1985 was to obtain a list of all individuals whose residences were in the take area for the dam, defined by the Army Corps of Engineers as all of the land below the 1365-foot contour. Surprisingly, there was no such list. A compilation made by the corps was inadequate since it listed just the names of land owners and included both those who lost only land and those who lost their homes. Only by conducting a parcel-by-parcel and house-by-house search, a suggestion made by Cornelius Abrams Jr., director of the Maps and Boundary Department for the Nation, was it possible to determine which land was actually within the take area and who was relocated. This proved extremely useful because it also demonstrated why certain people were often mentioned as relocatees when, in fact, they did not have to move. In several cases, although nearly all of an individual's land was taken, the house remained because it lay several feet above the contour. The maps were used as the final criterion of relocatee status in those cases where house location was in question.

A more serious problem was the determination of household composition since removal took place over several years, during which time the population fluctuated as people were born, died, were removed, or went away to school or the military. DuWayne Bowen, a relocatee who worked in the Maps and Boundary Department, was invaluable at this stage in providing information on spouses, children, kin, and nonrelatives living in particular houses. Asking individual Senecas to help in checking and rechecking the evolving list met with eager responses, often prompting spontaneous descriptions of life at both the "old places" and the relocation sites as well as suggestions of other useful reviewers. In general, there was a surprising degree of agreement in identifying relocatees. However, in cases where conflict arose, the word of the individual involved was taken as paramount, followed by that of family members and neighbors. While this leaves some margin of error, particularly since there is a kind of informal status associated with having been removed (a fact noted by Oliver-Smith [1986] for survivors of the Yungay, Peru, earthquake), it is minimal.

Children who were away at school were automatically included, as were those in hospitals or jails. Those in the military were placed on a separate list but included in the final total. Renters presented another difficult problem, since a series of families often occupied a house during the removal period. These individuals also faced greater hardships at this time because they were eligible for neither land nor a replacement house. Determinations about names to include followed the same pattern as previously described for home owners, except that if the individual or a co-resident could not be located, the word of the house owner was taken as paramount.

This research demonstrates conclusively that the previous counts of relocatees (Senate 1964, 18; Fenton 1967, 7; Hauptman 1986a, 88) significantly underestimated the impact of the dam on the Allegany population. Rather than the oft-quoted 130 families, or 482 individuals, there were actually 160 families, or 537 individuals, forced to remove. Thirteen men in the military during removal bring the total to 550. An additional 98 individuals lost much of their land, and 26 estates of deceased Senecas were destroyed. Even though this count includes non-Seneca spouses, it is still probably low because it does not include the Seneca spouses and children of military personnel who planned to return to Allegany nor family members of individual landowners whose rights to inheritance were eliminated.

The source of previous underestimates is clear. Walter Fuhriman (1963, 13), in a survey of the reservation prior to removal, reported 124 households within the take area and noted that all members of an additional six households were absent at the time of the study. The total resident population of Allegany as of 30 June 1962 was 1,103, of whom approximately 23 percent were absent (12). Fuhriman clearly stated that his figures were low; others have chosen to ignore his caveat. Except when referring specifically to his data, the more accurate figures will be used throughout this book.

Undercounts of potential or actual relocatees are common (Cernea and Guggenheim 1994, xiii), and while they may be due to methodological difficulties, they also serve to diminish the social impact of resettlement and lower the costs, thereby making projects more acceptable to the public or funding agencies. A parallel situation exists among the Navajo, where estimates of potential relocatees by the Navajos resulted in a number twice that determined by the Navajo–Hopi Indian Relocation Commission. The difference in numbers, according to Emily Benedek (1993, 339), was because the Navajos counted people rather than holders of grazing permits. Even if people are counted accurately, there is no guarantee that their ideas or feelings will be understood. As Robert Chambers (1991, 516) points out, "When people are taken into account, they are more often counted than listened to or learned from."

Previous visits to the reservation had established a small network of friends and acquaintances. Residence at the Highbanks Campground, owned and operated by the Nation and located just outside the Steamburg relocation site, facilitated extended personal visits and participation in many reservation activities, including sports events, public meetings, and Longhouse ceremonies. Attendance at the latter was encouraged by the late Richard Johnny-John, speaker for the animal moiety of the Coldspring Longhouse. This was important because, within the past decade, non-Indians had been refused entrance to the Longhouse or asked to leave. For the followers of Handsome Lake, scientific study of their religion and ceremonies is considered sacrilege. Out of respect for their beliefs and gratitude for their welcome, despite what must have been strong initial misgivings, these topics will not be dealt with except to cite previously reported, publicly available sources directly related to removal (cf. Abrams 1967; Austin 1986).

Informal interviews began with friends, campground employees, and Seneca Nation Library staff, and concentrated on recollections of pre- and post-removal life as well as reflections on the changes in the social, political, and religious structure of the reservation. These were conducted from a sample that cut across gender, age, religion, and political affiliation. Friends on both sides of the evolving Expressway issue spoke openly of their convictions and motivations, thereby eliminating bias on this critical issue. Frequently these interviews led to suggestions of other sources, including introductions. The latter were extremely important in opening communication with individuals holding strongly negative views of anthropologists. Once word of the research spread, several Senecas themselves initiated contact and offered their aid. To a great extent these were people who had long maintained an interest in the removal and enjoyed being able to reminisce and analyze. Additionally, their interests had led them to collect or retain news clippings and documents that otherwise might have been unavailable. Very rarely was there an attempt to manipulate or interpret data for personal advancement or justification of political ideology. Concomitantly, searches of public records in the Allegany branch of the SNI Library identified people who played significant roles in the period from 1956 to 1986, and special effort was made to interview these individuals.

Formal interviews were held with Senecas who occupied major elective or appointed positions. These were usually set up by appointment and centered on a relatively standard set of questions relating to the person's role, problems associated with it, and analysis of the effectiveness of particular policies and programs. These were usually followed by additional informal discussions.

Brief life histories were obtained from three individuals, although often extensive fragments of other life histories were provided in the course of the interviews. Those collected were from two individuals who were children or adolescents at the time of removal and one elder from the Longhouse.

A formal questionnaire might have provided more quantitative data, but residence on the reservation quickly demonstrated the inappropriateness of this method, as previously noted by Paul Feldsher (1970, 6) and Thomas McElwain (1978, 15–16). A social scientist with an armful of forms would have been as welcome as Dracula at a blood bank. This is true even if the researcher is Seneca (John 1989, 119), though to a lesser extent. In relating a painful experience, personal contact and the empathy of the listener are most important. Only after personal relationships were established was it possible for relocatees to discuss their experiences. The emotional context of tears and triumphs cannot be readily reduced to even an open-ended type of question.

The Allegany branch of the SNI Library contains a nearly complete set of the *Kinzua Planning Newsletter*, which began publication in 1961 to coordinate response to the dam threat and which later kept the community informed about the removal. This was succeeded in 1967 by *Oh-He-Yoh-Noh* (Allegheny People), a newsletter for the Allegany Reservation, including social and political notes, drawings, and commentary. Together these allowed a month-by-month reconstruction of the removal and post-removal period, indicating the rise and fall of social clubs, self-help groups, political organizations, community activities, Longhouse ceremonies and festivities, and the expanding political organization, including election results and committee assignments. The official SNI Newsletter provided more political information, such as synopses of council meetings, reports of official visits by SNI personnel to Albany and Washington, and accounts of their attempts to initiate new programs and obtain federal funding. The correspondence of Walter Taylor, the representative of the Philadelphia Yearly Meeting of Friends to the Senecas, and Merrill Bowen, president of the Cornplanter Landowners' Corporation, editor of the *Kinzua Planning Newsletter*, and later clerk of the Seneca Nation, also proved invaluable. These letters, which belonged to Bowen, were given by his heirs to the Cornplanter Descendants Association Archives.

In their entirety, these documents provide a chronology of events and emotions rarely, if ever, encountered in the study of forced relocation. One caveat must be noted. This is especially apparent in the first decade of *Oh-He-Yoh-Noh*, in which the dominance of the political beliefs and social interests of the editor is apparent; therefore, it should not be assumed that these reflect community consensus. The fact that dissent was expressed via this medium does, however, give an indication of the range of opinions, though not its depth. It reflects well on the openness of the editors in providing a forum and occasionally modifying their own views in the process. On the other hand, the length of the issues (four to twelve single-spaced pages), plus the fact that the newsletters were sustained solely by voluntary financial contributions, suggests strongly that they did, in fact, represent the views of a significant segment of the population, if not a majority.

The changing role of the Allegany communities vis-à-vis the larger sociopolitical spectrum was documented by a survey of the *Republican Press*, the white-owned and -operated daily newspaper in the city of Salamanca, located entirely within the Allegany Reservation. *The Warrior*, yearbook of Salamanca High School, was reviewed to determine the changing participation of young Senecas in the activities of the primarily white high school. Many of these yearbooks were loaned by their owners and contained comments by friends and acquaintances providing insights into intergroup tensions and prejudices, often denied or repressed by the individuals themselves. Although such comments obviously reflect the personalities of the individuals involved, thereby making extrapolation hazardous, common themes were apparent regardless of the gender of the owner or the years he or she attended the school. Further data on the academic and social activities of school students were obtained in documents prepared by the SNI Education Department (Fellows 1982) and in interviews with teachers, counselors, and administrators, both current and at the time of removal.

Academic commitments necessitated my leaving Highbanks in

September, but I returned in each of the next two summers and maintained close contacts in the intervening years by phone calls and visits. Three decades after removal, the event still resonates strongly among the relocatees and their children, many of whom were born following relocation. Although power has shifted to a new generation, as predicted by Scudder and Colson, and the communities have developed, the ghosts of that time remain. For young Senecas, this takes the form of increased distrust of federal and state government and determination that no more laws be broken. Older relocatees still wander through evening mists down to the reservoir banks to be near where the "old places" used to be. Grief is still strong beneath the surface, and any lengthy discussion is likely to prompt tearful recollections. In the words of DuWayne Bowen, "This is still our home. . . . It's just that we don't live here anymore."

THE SCUDDER-COLSON MODEL AS A FRAMEWORK

The initial formulation of the model used in this study was based upon field research conducted by Thayer Scudder and Elizabeth Colson among the fifty-seven thousand Gwembe Tonga who were relocated in 1957–58 because of construction of Kariba Dam on the Zambezi River in Zambia. When they began fieldwork in 1956, the project was designed to consist of a one-year pre-relocation baseline study and a follow-up post-relocation examination several years later. The second phase was completed in 1962–63, but they ultimately decided to continue the study indefinitely (Scudder 1993, 127).

The model proposed by Scudder and Colson (1982) has continued to evolve (Scudder 1993, 1997) based on increasingly long-term data supplied by the project, which now includes a new generation of students. It has stimulated a significant body of research and is at least partly responsible for the greatly increased attention given by the World Bank to the human costs of relocation. The case study of the Allegany Senecas was designed to see if a model derived from an agricultural Third World society would be useful in describing an involuntary relocation in the United States.

The model begins with the first government plans for a project that will necessitate the dislocation of people and ends when power shifts to a new generation born in the relocation site(s) and responsibility for the people and area shifts to local authorities. It has usually consisted of four stages (Scudder and Colson 1982; Scudder 1997), but Scudder (1993) briefly considered a five-stage model. While the number of stages and their designation has fluctuated based on new data from Zambia and elsewhere, the overall outline has remained stable. Because most relocations are unsuccessful and new communities are either not established or have become grossly dysfunctional, long-term studies of surviving relocation communities are important because they shed light on the least known stages of the process. The model of relocation briefly described below is expanded in chapter 2 and its utility is assessed in the conclusion.

The beginning of the resettlement process occurs when a government decides to undertake a development project. Dam construction is the single largest cause of involuntary relocation (Cernea and Guggenheim 1994, 2/6). Those whose homes and land will be lost are usually unaware of what is occurring, and their concerns and interests are not addressed; their first knowledge of impending removal may be when project construction begins. The initial reactions of the population are conservative, often to the extent of denying the existence of any threat.

As people are removed to new areas, often without appropriate facilities such as housing and potable water, they experience stress on several levels: physical (increased morbidity and mortality), psychological (trauma, guilt, grief, anxiety), and sociocultural (loss of key institutions, leadership, cultural symbols). Conservative responses continue as families turn to kin and co-ethnics for aid in coping. In some groups, adjustment and adaptation never occur, and relocation fails. In others, a few relocatees increase their social and economic risk taking, trying new crops or taking new jobs. In successful resettlements, this behavior is adopted by the majority of households, and a sense of community develops. People begin to identify with the new geographic features, develop associations to meet changed social needs, and emphasize the importance of education for their children.

The process is completed when those children reach adulthood and take over responsibility for community affairs. In order for this to occur, the children must have acquired the appropriate skills and knowledge and the government or agency in charge of the relocation must be willing to hand over authority to the new generation.

I lived at Allegany as the new generation was beginning its ascent to power. Although most members were born prior to removal, most of their childhood and all of their adolescence were spent in the new communities, and they were able to describe the continuing impact of removal on their lives. The births of their own children brought into stark contrast the experience of childhood by the two generations. Attacks on the Seneca land base in the 1980s permitted a comparison of the ways in which the generations mobilized to meet new threats and demonstrated the extent to which the Allegany Senecas and the Seneca Nation itself had established a strong presence in a larger social, political, and economic system.

The Allegany Senecas and Kinzua Dam

ONE

The Allegany Senecas

Shortly before noon on Saturday, 24 September 1994, present and former residents of the Allegany Reservation of the Seneca Nation of Indians came together at the Seneca Theater in Salamanca, New York, to commemorate the thirtieth anniversary of the relocation of over six hundred people from their homes and land on the banks of the Allegheny River. This was in accord with a resolution passed by the Tribal Council of the Seneca Nation sitting in Special Session on 5 September 1984, which proclaimed the last Saturday in September as "'Remember the Removal Day' in tribute to all the Seneca families who were removed from their homeland; and in remembrance of a great tragedy inflicted upon the Seneca People as a whole . . . in hopes that we shall never forget and that it will never happen again."

What follows is the story of that removal and the long-term effects it has had on the Seneca Nation and its people, particularly those of the Allegany Reservation. It represents not only original documents, newsletters, and other media accounts of the relocation, but also recollections of those who endured those difficult times and their reflections on how their lives have changed. The thirtieth anniversary marks a shift in generations, and in fact, the 1994 remembrance was significantly different from previous ones, in part because it coincided with the two hundredth anniversary of the Treaty of 1794, signed at Canandaigua, New York, which guaranteed the Senecas' land. Following a traditional opening, the Remember the Removal Day program began with a lecture and slide presentation on the Treaty of 1794, followed by the video presentation "This Loss of Land," a production of WCAU-TV in Philadelphia that was broadcast during the Nation's struggle in the early 1960s.

The focal point was the public premiere of "Lands of Our Ancestors," a retrospective film by Allen and Jadwiga Forbes documenting the last days in what Allegany residents refer to as "the old places." Although production of the film was funded by the Seneca Nation, very few people had seen it, but rumors of its strong emotional content filled the theater. It was introduced by George Heron, president of the Seneca Nation at the time of removal and still an important person within the Nation. Overcome by emotion as he began to recall the old times, he asked the projectionist to begin the film. The film opened as it ended, with Seneca children at the Indian School at Red House singing "America." Responses ranged from outbreaks of laughter and giggles, as now middle-aged people saw themselves as children in the film, to silence broken only by muffled sounds of crying as the audience watched belongings being loaded into trucks and torches being put to homes.

It is clear that the people of Allegany have succeeded in their new homes and that the Seneca Nation is now far stronger than it was thirty years ago. But the people have not forgotten—not the land, not the homes, not those who are no longer present. The lobby of the theater was filled with pots of chrysanthemum plants, each bearing the name of someone who had been relocated. All visitors were urged to take a pot home with them to plant as a living memorial to those who had gone before. Sad reflection rather than anger was the dominant emotion, and a quiet determination that this would never happen again was pervasive.

As I planted a yellow mum in memory of DeForrest Abrams in my garden, I too remembered how much had changed since I first went to live at Allegany ten years earlier. Many of those present at the first Remember the Removal Day were gone, and even some of the young people who had organized it now had streaks of gray in their hair.

The Senecas have fared far better than many groups forced to relocate. They have maintained a sense of community and have successfully established two relocation sites whose residents show no greater levels of social dysfunction than those in nearby non-Indian communities. For middle- and upper-class Americans, the idea of relocation is often associated with advancements in status or income, a new job, or improved living conditions for a family or individual. Although recognizing that this will entail a disruption of current routines, some logistical difficulties, and a period of readjustment, people see these as temporary impediments to a more rewarding future. The person most enthusiastic about a move is usually the one who will receive the most direct benefit, usually the one whose employment has changed. Children, who presumably benefit indirectly from increased family income, are often far less excited and may, in fact, be actively opposed, even if rarely in a position to affect the actual decision. Spouses, more likely to participate in decision making, are often more accepting than enthusiastic about relocating. Weissman and Paykel noted the depression seen in wives of new Yale faculty members uprooted from their former homes and the lack of similar data on the effects of relocation on children (cited in Scudder 1997, 686).

The relocation of the Senecas differs from this scenario in that an entire group was displaced and the impetus for removal came from the federal government, despite the loud objections of nearly the entire population. Most groups forced to relocate are politically powerless ethnic or cultural minorities (Scudder and Colson 1982, 268), and the experience often results not only in increased dysfunction at the individual or family level but also in the complete disintegration and collapse of the community. Lacking access to economic and political power, women in these groups usually fare worse than men (Scudder 1991, 178; Otten 1986, 108–9). There are virtually no data on the impact of resettlement on children, either from direct observation or secondary reports by parents. At the sociocultural level, the loss of important cultural symbols in the new environment adds more stress and may contribute to abrupt changes in leadership. The stages and effects of relocation are developed more fully in the following chapter, but underlying this research were two hypotheses on the long-term effects of removal on residents of the Allegany Reservation.

The major hypothesis was that Seneca women were more negatively affected by forced removal than Seneca men. Few relocation studies have directly addressed gender difference in adjustment, although Anita Spring's (1982) study of Angolan refugees in Zambia suggested that women fared better than men because they were able to improve both their economic and social status through marriage to higher-class Zambian men. Mariel Otten (1986, 108–9) noted that women were denied official status as "transmigrants" (relocatees) in Indonesia. Removal weakened their position because it undermined traditional female support networks and forced them to assume a disproportionate amount of agricultural work.

I believed that the traditional role of Iroquois women as "mothers of the nation" and holders of land titles, enhanced by matrilineal descent, would place additional stress on women at Allegany because they were prohibited both from voting and holding political office in the Seneca Nation at the time of removal (Bilharz 1995; Bilharz and Abler 1996). Therefore, the base of female unity was eliminated through processes in which female interests could be addressed and acted upon only by informal means, such as pressure on husbands and other male relatives.

The second hypothesis concerned sociocultural adaptation and suggested the Longhouse—originally a residence for a matrilineage, later adopted as the symbol of the Iroquois Confederacy, and currently the "church" of the followers of Handsome Lake—would emerge as a political symbol of Seneca unity and Iroquois identity. This could be demonstrated by noting Christian attendance at major Longhouse rites, such as the Strawberry and Green Corn Dances and Midwinter Rites. Preliminary confirmation of this was suggested by a statement in the *New York Times* on 10 June 1962 by De-Forest Billy, tribal councilor during the dam fight, who said, "All Senecas are followers of Handsome Lake, in a sense. You always have a little of that in you no matter whether you go to the Baptist Church or not." It was expected that the sanction of Longhouse leaders would become increasingly important in debates over issues confronting the Nation and that they would be viewed by both Senecas and non-Indians as the ultimate arbiters in matters of tradition and cultural reformulation at the relocation sites. The Longhouse would also remind Senecas of the former strength and glory of the Confederacy at the time when it held the balance of power between competing European nations in North America and would provide solace when the relative impotence of the Seneca Nation vis-à-vis the federal government was a constant presence.

During the course of field research, a third hypothesis evolved that related the emotional trauma and stress felt by children to their level of political activism as adults. Young people in their twenties who stridently opposed the completion of the Southern Tier Expressway through the reservation tended to report the most grief, fear, and disruption at the time of removal. Although there was no evidence to suggest that they actually experienced more stress than their peers, the emotional impact of removal was far greater on them. The lack of contemporary data on the responses of children, the contradictory reports of parents and children, and the unexpected development of this issue made it impossible to adequately test this hypothesis, but the evidence strongly suggests a correlation and demonstrates the need for increased attention to impacts on children in future relocation studies.

THE ALLEGANY SENECAS BEFORE KINZUA DAM

The Senecas are an Iroquoian-speaking people whose historic homeland is the area between the Genesee River and Canandaigua Lake in western New York (Abler and Tooker 1978, 505). The 1687 French expedition under Denonville destroyed four major Seneca villages and resulted in the geographic division of the tribe into two territorial clusters, the eastern Senecas in two villages in the area of Lake Canandaigua and the western Senecas in two villages along the Genesee River (507). George Abrams (1976, 20) suggests this invasion may have been responsible for the first permanent Seneca settlement along the Allegheny River.

By the early eighteenth century the western Senecas were moving farther west into the Ohio Valley. Michael McConnell (1992, 19) argues that this migration can be viewed as a resettlement of ancestral territory because Erie and Monogahelan captives may have been the vanguard for movement south from Niagara. Taken as captives in the 1680s, these nominal Senecas, Cayugas, and Onondagas may have remembered their old home territories and thus facilitated the occupation of these lands by the western Senecas. Regardless of whether they followed an overland route from the Genesee Valley to the headwaters of the Allegheny or moved south along the Lake Erie plain toward Cuyahoga and Sandusky, they were "moving into lands that, by their standards, they could legitimately claim as a result of the Erie war" (19). In 1750 Pennsylvania governor James Hamilton noted that the Iroquois in Ohio Country were more numerous than those in the areas they left (20).

Although the movement reflected increasing colonial pressure, the Senecas arrived along the Allegheny River and in the Ohio Valley as the result of conscious, planned decisions and not as refugee populations (McConnell 1992, 24). Unlike the Seneca experience nearly two centuries later, this was a voluntary removal in which Seneca interests played the dominant role. Like their Allegany descendants, they forged a new identity within the context of a new location.

By 1779 at least some Seneca displacement was involuntary and resulted from General Sullivan's burning of the Genesee towns and Colonel Brodhead's sacking of Indian settlements along the Allegheny River (A. Wallace 1969, 168). Among those affected at this time was Cornplanter, who, along with his half-brother Handsome Lake, would play an important role at the turn of the century.

Seneca responses to historical developments, including removals, are best viewed within the context of the Iroquois Confederacy or Five Nations. Formed prior to European contact, the Confederacy was an attempt to eliminate internecine raiding and warfare among the Senecas, Cayugas, Onondagas, Oneidas, and Mohawks. In the early eighteenth century when the Tuscaroras moved to Iroquoia from the Carolinas, it became known as the Six Nations, although the Tuscaroras never sat as chiefs on the Confederacy Council, their interests instead represented by the Oneidas. Each Nation passed down orally its own version of the founding of the League, so there are minor variations in the accounts (Parker 1968; Noon 1949; Gibson 1992). The only complete written version in an Iroquoian language (Onondaga) was dictated to Alexander Goldenweiser in 1912 by John Arthur Gibson. It has recently been published in both an English translation by Hanni Woodbury, Reg Henry, and Harry Webster and the original Onondaga (Gibson 1992). This founding epic illustrates Iroquois values and gives insight into sociocultural and political responses of historic and contemporary Senecas.

According to the Gibson version, an Iroquois woman received a dream message from the Creator foretelling the birth to her daughter of a son who would be sent by the Great Spirit to deliver the Good Message of Power, Peace, and the Great Law. Having first given the message to his mother and grandmother, Dekanawidah, the founding culture hero, journeyed to the Mohawks' settlement, where he converted a cannibal and conferred upon him the title of Hiawatha. Together the two men set out to spread the word among the other Iroquois tribes. Using skillful diplomacy, they slowly built their ranks of support to surround the recalcitrant Onondaga wizard Tadodaho, and in reciprocity for his acceptance of the Great Law, the Onondagas were made the Fire Keepers for the League.

The League itself was conceptualized as a single family and symbolized by a longhouse, the traditional residence of a matrilineage. Within the longhouse, each tribe had its own fire, as would each daughter, thus maintaining a significant degree of independence over its own internal affairs. The Senecas, demographically largest and westernmost of the tribes, were made Keeper of the Western Door, and all messages from that direction were to be delivered to the Iroquois Confederacy through them. On the opposite end, the Mohawks became the Keeper of the Eastern Door. Perhaps in recognition of both their size and military reputation, the Senecas also provided the League with its two war chiefs.

The League was governed by fifty chiefs, who held titles vested in matrilineages. Chiefs were chosen and removed for cause by the members of the matrilineages through the actions of the adult women. This recognition of female authority reflected the fact that it was women who first accepted the message of Dekanawidah and Hiawatha. The matrilineal inheritance of chiefly titles and the symbolic use of the longhouse for the League emphasizes the important role played by women in Iroquois society. Although unable to serve as chiefs, women could bring Confederacy proceedings to a halt if a vacancy existed and they refused to nominate a replacement chief. Since all would potentially suffer in such a situation, the League's political system required gender complementarity despite the fact that men and women had different roles (Bilharz 1995).

Another source of female political authority was the dominant role women held in deciding whether to adopt or sacrifice war captives. As Iroquois warriors were reduced in numbers by prolonged "mourning wars" and skirmishes with invading Europeans, adoption became important economically and politically. This would have been more important for the Senecas confronting both westward-moving French and English and hostile tribes to the west and especially south.

Traditional Iroquois male roles often required significant periods of absence—on winter hunts, military raids, or diplomatic missions. Vesting control over land and subsistence in females again demonstrated the importance of reciprocity and complementarity as Iroquois values and enhanced the status of women. While unable to force their male relatives and mates to go on the warpath, women could create a favorably militant atmosphere by constant reminders of unavenged deaths or could dampen martial ardor by refusing to relinquish food supplies for exploits they deemed unwise.

Iroquois subsistence was based on the "Three Sisters"—maize, beans, and squash—still important elements in Seneca cuisine. Initial clearing of the land was done by men, with subsequent planting, weeding, and harvesting done by groups of related women. Male contributions were significant and included the products of the hunt, especially deer, for both meat and hides. Later, with increasing pressure from Euro-American settlers and dependence on trade goods, male activities became an important source of barter goods and eventually cash for items such as cloth, metal pots, guns, and ammunition. While physically taxing, women's horticultural roles were made bearable, and even pleasant, by the existence of communal work groups that allowed a degree of flexibility for individual women temporarily slowed by illness or childbirth. Mary Jemison (Seaver 1990), the "White Woman of the Genesee" who was captured by Delawares as a girl and later given to the Senecas, compared the lives of Iroquois women favorably to those of their isolated white neighbors and chose not to return to the society of her birth.

European invasions caused significant changes in Iroquois society, changes initially felt most strongly by men. The nature of the League shifted from primary concern with internal harmony to confronting external threats, which also endangered Iroquois unity by pitting Iroquois nations against one another as they struggled to control trade throughout the Mohawk, Susquehanna, and Ohio Valleys. Hostilities with non-Iroquois Indians also increased due to competition between European nations in North America.

League unity was irreparably broken at the Battle of Oriskany in 1777 when Senecas and Mohawks fought with the Crown and Oneidas with the rebels of Tryon County, New York. This would eventually result in the creation of two confederacies in the post-Revolutionary period, one centered in Canada on the Grand River in Ontario, to which Joseph Brant had fled with many Loyalist Iroquois, and the other at Onondaga, near Syracuse, New York, which became the focus for Iroquois in the newly formed United States.

This period was one of increasing disillusion among many Iroquois groups and can best be illustrated by considering the case of the Senecas along the Allegheny River. As noted, men were first to feel the impact of change. No longer were they feared as powerful warriors, their diplomatic skills were no longer required or recognized as the U.S. government treated the Iroquois as conquered nations, and the rewards of hunting were greatly reduced as forests fell to expanding roads and towns. Although dependent on foreign trade goods for well over a century, Iroquois women still maintained control of their lives, planted and reaped their harvests, and raised their children. But even for them, the changes, though less direct, were apparent.

In October 1784 representatives of the Six Nations met with U.S. officials at Fort Stanwix, which resulted in a treaty guaranteeing the territory of the pro-U.S. Oneidas and Tuscaroras and ceding Seneca lands in western New York and Pennsylvania. Competition for former Confederacy land occurred between states as well as companies of land speculators. As Indians in the Ohio Country began to wage attacks on new frontier settlements, the federal government changed its policy of claiming Indian land by right of conquest (Prucha 1962, 44) and instead offered compensation to the tribes for lands previously ceded. It was particularly important to deal with the Iroquois since the government in Philadelphia did not want experienced Seneca warriors joining the tribes in the Ohio Valley.

Despite the treaty, incursions on remaining Indian land continued; in 1790 the Seneca chief Cornplanter, along with Big Tree and Halftown, traveled to Philadelphia to complain to President George

Washington of white encroachment on Seneca lands. Washington, in a letter dated December 1790, guaranteed the Senecas' boundaries and control of their lands. At this time Cornplanter asked the president to recommend men to serve as teachers to the Senecas, and Washington suggested the Quakers. Cornplanter's request appears in the minutes of the Philadelphia Yearly Meeting of Friends of 21 April 1791. In June the Quakers agreed to take and educate three boys, including Cornplanter's son Henry (Deardorff and Snyderman 1956, 584).

The next year the Iroquois and the hostile Ohio tribes held a council at Buffalo Creek. Cornplanter, this time with the backing of the matrons, urged support of the federal government, and the League agreed with him. His offer to go to Ohio as mediator was accepted, and in 1792 he and an Iroquois delegation met with the western Indians. The Shawnees, perhaps recalling previous Iroquois land dealings, accused Red Jacket and Cornplanter of cowardice. Another attempt at mediation in 1793 was also fruitless (A. Wallace 1969, 164–65).

In the meantime, white inroads into Iroquois lands increased, and in an effort to keep restless Seneca warriors from joining Tecumseh and the Ohio tribes, Washington sent Colonel Timothy Pickering to meet with the Six Nations at Canandaigua. Fifty-nine sachems and war chiefs of the Six Nations, including the Senecas Cornplanter and Handsome Lake, attended. Cornplanter had been of great help to the new U.S. government, and the Commonwealth of Pennsylvania had also recognized his contribution by granting him three mile-square tracts on the upper Allegheny, lands known as the Cornplanter Grant, which would also be inundated in 1965 by Kinzua Dam. Despite Cornplanter's experience with the Americans, and perhaps because of Red Jacket's denunciation of the large land cessions and sales he had made to them, the Senecas requested the advice of the Philadelphia Yearly Meeting of Friends, better known as Quakers. Four Friends made the eight-day trip to Canandaigua, two of whom kept diaries of their journey. It is interesting to note that, although requested to sign the treaty by one of the Senecas, Farmer's Brother, the Quakers refused to do so, feeling that the Indians were not adequately compensated for their lands (Senate 1964, 131). The Canandaigua Treaty of 1794, also known as the

Pickering Treaty after Timothy Pickering, states in Article 3:
"Now, the United States acknowledge all the land within the afore-
mentioned boundaries, to be the property of the Seneka nation; and
the United States will never claim the same, nor disturb the Seneka
Nation, nor any of the Six Nations, or of their Indian friends resid-
ing thereon and united with them, in the free use and enjoyment
thereof; but it shall remain theirs, until they choose to sell the same
to the people of the United States, who have the right to purchase."
The impact of both the Pickering Treaty and Cornplanter's meetings with George Washington would reverberate two centuries later
as the Seneca Nation confronted the federal government using Article 3 as the cornerstone of their fight against Kinzua Dam.

Despite the beliefs of many Senecas and their supporters, the
treaty was signed by Pickering, *not* by Washington, although this
conviction would appear to underlie the prominent position Washington holds in the Seneca worldview. Washington did, however,
exchange speeches with Cornplanter and promised the Indians access to the federal courts to prevent white incursions, so Seneca
faith in him was not totally misplaced. Nevertheless, Washington's
own motives for seeking peace may have been influenced as much
by his personal land speculation in the Ohio Valley as by national
politics.

More important than Washington in the long term was the association between the Allegany Senecas and the Philadelphia Yearly
Meeting of Friends. The Quaker-Indian association has a long history in the northeast, with relations between the two groups being
generally good. Between 1676 and 1755 there were no Indian wars in
those colonies with strong Quaker influence (James 1963, 91). In
1687 the Burlington, New Jersey, Quarterly Meeting of Friends began a special campaign to convert the Indians, and George Fox himself urged Quakers in the colonies to report successes in conver-
sion, particularly of Indian leaders, to the London Yearly Meeting. It
was believed that Indians would provide confirmation of the Quaker
doctrine of "inner light" through discovery of their past or present
illumination by Christ, found preserved in traditional lore (91–93).

The first formal organization to aid Indians was set up in 1756 by
Israel Pemberton of the Philadelphia Yearly Meeting. It can be interpreted as an attempt to redeem the Quaker ideal of pacifism under

attack during the French and Indian War by stopping Indian raids
without the use of the military. The Friendly Association for Re-
gaining and Preserving Peace with the Indians by Pacific Measures
failed to get official recognition by the Society of Friends (Deardorff
and Snyderman 1956, 583), but its membership eventually formed
the core of the Indian Affairs Committee of the Philadelphia Yearly
Meeting set up in 1795, a committee that was made permanent the
following year (585–86) and that was the major outside support organization for the Seneca Nation in its fight against Kinzua Dam in
the 1960s.

The tradition of Quaker representation at treaty negotiations began with the Friendly Association, whose main purpose was to
force colonial officials to make peace with the Indians. Pemberton
felt that the land issue was most important and that unless Indians
felt secure in their land base, it was useless to pursue other interests
(James 1963, 190). In Pennsylvania the lieutenant governors could
not hold treaties without members of the Friendly Association in
attendance and overseeing the proceedings (179). The Quaker desire
to deal with individual groups within the borders of Pennsylvania
ran counter to Sir William Johnson's policy of dealing with the Six
Nations, and after 1762 the association was reduced to giving gifts
to Indians visiting Philadelphia (191). That Quaker interest in Indians was strongly motivated by a desire to keep peace rather than
by a deep-seated concern for the indigenous inhabitants is demonstrated by Quaker apathy toward them once border raids ceased
(190).

Attempts to establish long-term missions among the Senecas
had been unsuccessful for the most part until 1798, when the Quakers, several of whom had been present at the Canandaigua negotiations, arrived to teach the "arts of civilization." The 1790s saw much
speculation in former Seneca territory, and when Robert Morris
sold much of it to the Holland Land Company in 1796, the company
insisted that Indian title be extinguished before the transaction was
finalized. Morris asked Washington to appoint a commissioner to
preside at a treaty conference to arrange for the purchase, fearing
that a direct approach to the Senecas about land cessions at a time
when the Indians of the Ohio Valley were at war with the United
States might be sufficient to bring Seneca warriors into the conflict.

The eventual treaty meeting, held in 1797 at Big Tree, brought together representatives of the Holland Land Company, the federal government, Robert Morris's son Thomas, and over one thousand Senecas led by Red Jacket, Farmer's Brother, and Cornplanter (Chazanof 1970, 21). Although the Indians initially refused to sign the agreement, cash gifts totaling $1,150 from Morris and others, as well as the promise of annuities, were sufficient to change the Seneca perspective. On 15 September 1797, fifty-two Seneca leaders and Thomas Morris signed the Treaty of Big Tree, ceding the land to Robert Morris for one hundred thousand dollars. He in turn transferred the land to the Holland Land Company (22). Of their original four-hundred-thousand-acre domain, the Senecas now retained fewer than two hundred thousand acres in ten separate tracts, including two tracts of forty-two square miles each along the Cattaraugus Creek and the Allegheny River (Chazanof 1970, 22; Abler and Tooker 1978, 508).

With the Seneca land base severely eroded and traditional lifestyles under increasing pressure, two major factions emerged. Best known, probably because of their literacy and interaction with whites, are the groups led by Cornplanter in the United States and Brant in Canada, which advocated the adoption of some aspects of white culture. Impressed by the Quakers, Cornplanter sought assistance in such areas as developing agriculture and starting sawmills. Excess Seneca lands could be sold or leased and the income used to purchase the necessary equipment (A. Wallace 1969, 202–4). The opposite position was taken by the faction led by Red Jacket, which strongly defended traditional Seneca ways and opposed further land cessions and adoption of white culture. The increased factionalism became a major source of anxiety because it underscored the lack of effective leadership, and the anxiety was not relieved by the old religious rituals that emphasized indulgence in dependency wishes and aggressive fantasies (444–45).

The emergence of minor prophets and the revival of the white dog ceremony began in 1798 (A. Wallace 1969, 207; Abrams 1976, 52). In June 1799 Handsome Lake, Cornplanter's half-brother (his mother's son), had the first of his series of visions in which he met representatives of the Creator. As Anthony Wallace (1969, 239) has stated, these prophetic visions "articulated the dilemmas in which the Iroquois were trapped and prescribed both religious and secular solutions." Handsome Lake soon became a religious leader. His early gospel had a predominantly apocalyptic theme, stressing the imminence of world destruction, sin, and a prescription for salvation that has been interpreted as a response to social disorganization (A. Wallace 1969, 249; 1978, 446). Drawing upon age-old fears of witches, Handsome Lake dropped his initial concern with witchcraft when he was accused of using these charges to eliminate political rivals such as Red Jacket. Unlike Wallace, Elisabeth Tooker (1968) sees the Code of Handsome Lake (Fenton 1968) not as psychotherapy for a disorganized society but as a change from the old, individualistic values useful in a hunting society to new, communal values best suited to an agricultural society.

The social gospel of Handsome Lake evolved more slowly and, in general, supported the assimilationist views of Cornplanter. While favoring education for at least some Indian children, white material culture and agriculture, and the Quaker mission, he opposed further land alienation and government attempts to enlist Iroquois warriors in the War of 1812 (A. Wallace 1978, 447). The Christian influence on Handsome Lake is seen most strongly in his images of heaven and hell, but there is an emphasis on old Iroquois customs and ceremonies as well, such as the Strawberry Dance and other ceremonies reflecting the agricultural cycle.

Regardless of which interpretation is emphasized, there is no doubt that the Quaker influence and the difficulties of reservation life led to profound changes in major Seneca institutions. By the end of the eighteenth century life had changed radically for the Senecas.

Handsome Lake's social gospel, although emphasizing traditional male-female reciprocity, contained what Anthony Wallace (1969, 282) has described as a "revised domestic morality" in which women's customary roles in the domestic sphere were significantly reduced because the nuclear family was supposed to take precedence over matrilineal ties. Sons were to obey their fathers, who were to support their families through agricultural pursuits. Women were to take their proper role as housewives and cease interfering in the lives of their daughters. Indeed, Handsome Lake saw this as a central problem in Seneca life. From the beginning the Quakers had made no secret of their displeasure over seeing Indian women laboring in the fields while Indian men appeared idle (226), and Handsome Lake's revelations reflected this concern. By the time of his third vision on 5 February 1800, he had obtained the critical support of his half-sister, Gayantgogwus, and her husband, both of whom were well-respected medicine people. Gayantgogwus was particularly important because the angels entrusted her with making the medicine that would cure Handsome Lake's illness (248). The agreement of women was still important despite outside pressures.

Subsistence had changed to more male-oriented agriculture, which brought about radical changes in settlement patterns and the end of the traditional longhouse as a matrilineal residence (Abrams 1976, 54). The Quakers prevailed upon the Senecas to adopt single-family log and shingle farmhouses and fenced fields spread out along the river, which allowed men to undertake agricultural tasks, previously within the domain of women, out of sight of their neighbors (Fenton 1967, 2). Within a generation the transition from matrilineal household to nuclear family was complete, with families eventually becoming patrilineal with respect to name and inheritance (A. Wallace 1969, 312). Although women still held primary responsibility for children and the naming of chiefs, their roles were now also significantly compromised and the symbolic importance of the longhouse greatly reduced.

The importance of George Washington as a sacred symbol within the Iroquois belief system had its roots in the second of Handsome Lake's visions. On the evening of 8 August 1799, three representatives of the Creator and a guide took Handsome Lake on a sky journey and showed him heaven and hell. On this trip they encountered Washington, halfway to heaven, sitting on his porch with his dog and representing the good white man who guaranteed Indian land rights at Canandaigua (A. Wallace 1969, 244). A report of Handsome Lake's visions (which does not include the George Washington story) was written down by the Quaker teacher Henry Simmons (1799), who probably heard it directly from the prophet himself (A. Wallace 1969, 243). At a council called by Cornplanter, Simmons, when asked if he believed that the visions were true, responded that similar revelations were given to whites, and since all peoples were made by the great Spirit, there was no reason to disbelieve the visions, although he noted that Handsome Lake's actual recollection of the vision might not be complete due to its great length (A. Wallace 1952, 348). Simmons's measured answer, reflecting the Quaker doctrine of the "inner light," provided additional support for Handsome Lake.

Despite increased agricultural productivity, the introduction of spinning and weaving, and craft specialization, the Seneca land base was still not secure. In 1810 the Holland Land Company sold its preemptive rights to five Seneca reservations, including the Allegany, Cattaraugus, and Tonawanda Reservations, to the Ogden Land Company, and some Iroquois asked President James Madison about possible removal to the west (Abrams 1976, 55). In 1826 the Senecas sold the Ogden Land Company eighty-five thousand acres for $48,260 in a treaty signed at Buffalo Creek but never ratified by the Senate. At this time Joseph Elkington, a Quaker, implied that the traditional chiefs were corrupt and should be replaced by an elected government (57). The first Seneca constitution, written in a council at Buffalo Creek in June 1833, placed executive and legislative power in the chiefs and the headmen and provided for the deposition of anyone using alcohol or favoring removal to the west, a clear infringement on the traditional role of the matrons. Despite official urging to the contrary, six people left to explore the northwest Indian Territory set aside by Congress (60).

Factionalism continued and by 1835 centered on whether annuities should continue to be given to the chiefs for distribution or should instead go directly to family heads. In 1838, by means of forgery, bribery, and alcohol, the Ogden Land Company purchased all remaining Seneca land in New York, and the Senecas accepted a government offer of 1,824,000 acres in Kansas (Abrams 1976, 61). Only forty-three of the eighty-one to ninety-one chiefs signed the agreement; of these, sixteen were bribed and the others said they were threatened or their signatures were forged (Abler and Tooker 1978, 511). The exact number of chiefs is unknown because the factions were unable to agree on who the chiefs were (Thomas S. Abler, personal communication, 28 July 1997). The Senecas reported the events of the Buffalo Creek Council to the Quakers by letter in February 1838 and requested their aid. Four Senecas arrived in Philadelphia shortly thereafter as delegates of the Six Nations and, accompanied by four Quakers, continued on to Washington to address the president and Congress. In a memorial dated 12 March 1838 and signed by Thomas Wistar, clerk of the Philadelphia Yearly Meeting, the Quakers made the same appeal to the national honor as they would over a century later: "Shall a great and powerful nation, like the United States, rich in soil and in all its products, drive from the scanty pittance of land yet left them, these unresisting and helpless people, to gratify the cravings of avarice? Your memorialists trust not. They respectfully, but earnestly entreat you to withhold your sanction from this pretended treaty, and thus save from the stain of so disgraceful an act, the character of our beloved country" (Report of the Committee 1838, 21–22).

Despite these protests, the treaty was promulgated in 1840. The Quakers then retained the services of Daniel Webster and two other attorneys, who worked out a compromise treaty in 1842 under instructions from President John Tyler. This treaty negated the 1838 agreement, and the Senecas relinquished the Buffalo Creek and Tonawanda Reservations but retained the Allegany, Cattaraugus, and Oil Spring Reservations. The Seneca chiefs at Tonawanda refused to sign either agreement, and without Quaker support they had to look elsewhere for help. The anthropologist Lewis Henry Morgan and his secret fraternal society, the Grand Order of the Iroquois, offered aid and began to circulate petitions in January 1846 among the local citizens, many of whom, including Ontario County district attorney John Martindale, were outraged by the Ogden maneuvers. The long fight by the Tonawanda Senecas and Martindale, who became their attorney, resulted in the 1856 purchase of one-tenth of their former reservation from the Ogden Land Company (Abrams 1976, 62; Abler and Tooker 1978, 511; Tooker 1995). Any existing differences between the Senecas at Tonawanda and their fellow Iroquois at Allegany and Cattaraugus were no doubt exacerbated by this turn of events. More important in the long run was that fact that Morgan, as an anthropologist, took an active role in attempting to address what he felt were inequities in U.S. dealings with the Senecas. This role would be reprised a century later by William Fenton, Elisabeth Tooker, and others, working this time alongside Quakers from Philadelphia.

The annuities payment controversy continued. Despite congressional authorization for the president to distribute annuities to family heads, in the spring of 1848 payment was once again given to the chiefs, who decided to use a percentage of the money for the relief of poor Senecas and those suffering from a typhoid epidemic. This was interpreted by some Senecas as the chiefs' pocketing tribal estates. Senecas at Cattaraugus and Allegany asked the federal government to change the distribution method, and in November payments were made to family heads (Abrams 1976, 66–67; Abler and Tooker 1978, 511).

The modern Seneca Nation of Indians (SNI) was created on 4 December 1848 at a general convention on the Cattaraugus Reservation. Government by chiefs at Allegany and Cattaraugus was abolished and replaced by an elected council of eighteen (now sixteen) members and an executive branch consisting of president, clerk, and treasurer. The judicial office of peacemaker under the old chiefs' government was retained. A written constitution based on a text by tribal attorney Chester Howe was adopted. As a result of this major governmental change at Cattaraugus and Allegany, relations between these reservations and Tonawanda were severed (Abrams 1976, 67–68; Abler and Tooker 1978, 511–12). The constitution included a clause, suggested by the missionary Asher Wright, that no Seneca land could be sold without the consent of three-quarters of the "mothers of the nation" (Abler 1992, 28). Allegany and Cattaraugus were themselves divided into two new factions, the New Government Party and the Old Chiefs. In February 1849 Commissioner Medill recognized the Seneca Nation of Indians, and the New Government Party won election in May (Abler 1969, 109–46; Abrams 1976, 68; Abler and Tooker 1978, 512). Attempts over the next ten years to abolish the new form of government failed to achieve the necessary two-thirds majority.

By tradition, the president and treasurer are from different reservations, with the presidency shifting to the other reservation each election. The president and treasurer are considered the "heads" of their respective reservations. This has the effect of preventing a president from serving two consecutive terms. In eras of strong parties or alliances, the president and treasurer run for the other office in the next election, thus ensuring (if victorious) stability over at least a four-year period. The clerk is elected from the same reservation as the president, so the occupant of this office changes after each election.

The creation of the Seneca Nation of Indians in 1848 affected the Allegany and Cattaraugus Senecas in two ways. First, it necessarily resulted in the removal of their members from the circle of Confederacy chiefs at Onondaga; the Seneca titles were now held by members of the Tonawanda Band of Senecas. Although the Confederacy had no formal political role to fill, it still provided a framework for concerted action by Iroquois peoples throughout New York (Abler 1984, 89). The Seneca Nation would call upon and receive backing from the Confederacy in the 1960s, but their long-term isolation may well have tempered its speed and strength.

Second, the traditional role of women as critical players in the political arena was eliminated since there were no more chiefs to be appointed and overseen. Following nineteenth-century U.S. political tradition, women were denied the right to vote and hold office. The formal status of women in Iroquois society was therefore reduced, and like their white female neighbors, they saw political power concentrated in the hands of men. Unlike white women, however, the Senecas had one significant advantage. Despite the new form of government, membership in the Seneca Nation remained matrilineal. Unlike Seneca men, they were assured that their children would always be Senecas. They were still the "mothers of the nation." While the importance of this may not be readily apparent to people used to patrilineal inheritance, it provided a basis for female unity that could not be eroded by changing political or economic systems. Furthermore, the ancient tradition of female behind-the-scenes politicking remained and would be rapidly utilized as the still disenfranchised women organized themselves to once again fight against the taking of Seneca land for Kinzua Dam.

Although no land has been sold to whites since 1842 (the Senecas were specifically excluded from the Dawes Act), the Seneca land base was eroded by leases, beginning in the 1830s when railroads were built through the reservations on rented lands. Villages of whites grew up on land leased from both individual Senecas and the council. These villages were illegal since the required congressional confirmation was not obtained, but in 1875 Congress authorized six villages—Salamanca, Carrollton, West Salamanca, Vandalia, Great Valley, and Red House—comprising almost ten thousand acres or one-third of the Allegany Reservation, to be leased to whites for five years. In 1880 the leases were renewed for twelve years, and in 1892 they were renewed for ninety-nine years (Abler and Tooker 1978, 513). The fight by the Seneca Nation to address a century of unfair leasing practices, which is described in chapter 7, draws upon experiences during and after the Kinzua Dam crisis.

Despite land losses and unfair leases, many Senecas still followed the pattern of accommodation laid down by Cornplanter. This can be seen most obviously in Seneca participation in the Civil War. Although Seneca enlistees were often rejected initially, when the numbers of white recruits declined, they were welcomed eagerly. This represented the first real opportunity for Seneca males to re-create the traditional Iroquois role of honored warrior. Seneca elders at Allegany still vividly recall the pomp and ceremony surrounding the funeral of the last surviving Civil War veteran. But if Senecas were willing to make the ultimate sacrifice for the United States, it would be reasonable to expect commensurate treatment for the Seneca Nation from the federal government. After three major U.S. wars—World War I, World War II, and the Korean conflict—in which Senecas served with honor and distinction and the failure of both New York State and the federal government to address Indian grievances, it is not surprising that the opposition to Kinzua Dam resulted in the formation of a new political party whose core membership was composed of World War II and Korean War veterans. They now realized that the new arena for Iroquois warriors would be in the halls of Congress for the conscience of the American people rather than in the battlefields of Europe and Asia for ideals of democracy and freedom that often seemed not to apply to Indians. Scudder (1993, 139) has noted how threats of removal fostered new political alliances and leadership in Zambia and aided the African National Congress in its recruitment efforts.

From the Civil War to the post–World War II era, the men of the SNI Council met infrequently, sometimes only once a year, usually to approve agreements for oil, gas, or mineral exploration. Formally excluded from voting or holding office, women remained secure in their traditional roles as "mothers of the nation," and some moved into prominence on the national level. Most important of these was Alice Lee Jemison, who led the unsuccessful fight against the extension of New York state fish and game laws onto Seneca territory in the late 1920s and who was appointed as the Washington lobbyist against the Seneca Conservation Act of 1927 by the SNI Council (Hauptman 1981, 7, 45). Her activities were also important in turning the Seneca vote against the Indian Reorganization Act (Wheeler-Howard Act). Jemison spent a significant portion of her time involved with the American Indian Federation, and her program included the removal of John Collier as head of the Bureau of Indian Affairs, the abolition of the bureau itself, and the repeal of the Indian Reorganization Act (46).

Jemison personified a more public version of traditional behind-the-scenes maneuvering by Iroquois women. Her nomination for positions in the Indian service by the SNI Council presaged the appointment of large numbers of women to committees in the Kinzua era, and the fact that her uncle, Cornelius Seneca, was elected SNI president suggests her input, if not influence, on formal deliberations. She also reflects a more public reappearance of another traditional role of Iroquois women, that of influencing warfare. Unlike men who were willing to enlist or be drafted by the U.S. military, and who saw this as a valued performance of traditional male duty, Jemison argued for Seneca resistance to the Selective Service Act before World War II (Hauptman 1981, 39). While Jemison's actions clearly demonstrate the strong influence of traditional Iroquois gender roles, she was also part of a larger, growing, pan-Indian movement (Hertzberg 1971), many of whose origins were in the Indian boarding schools. (Jemison's Seneca mother and Cherokee father met at Hampton Institute; she was educated off the reservation and developed close ties with male and female political leaders in Buffalo.) In seeking support for Seneca and other Indian causes, she sometimes accepted aid from extreme right-wing groups whose Nazi sympathies were well known. For the story of Kinzua Dam, it is most useful to note that in addressing Seneca issues, Jemison emphasized the historic participation of the Senecas in the Six Nations Confederacy and the sovereignty guarantees in the Treaty of Canandaigua. Despite the fact that the SNI was no longer a part of the

Confederacy, Jemison saw no reason not to seek common cause with the Six Nations Council and placed Seneca issues within the broader contexts of the Confederacy and pan-Indian concerns. In the 1950s and 1960s, like Alice Lee Jemison, the Senecas would turn again to their historic ties to the Confederacy and seek its support.

Scientific interest in the Senecas, which began with the publication of Lewis Henry Morgan's *League of the Hau-de-nau-sau-nee, or Iroquois* in 1851, received a boost in 1935 when John Collier appointed William Duncan Strong as head of the new Applied Anthropology Staff of the Bureau of Indian Affairs (BIA). It was under the auspices of this program that many anthropologists received much of their early fieldwork experience. William Fenton, whose dissertation research had been done among the Senecas, was appointed as a community worker in the Indian Service at Tonawanda in 1935 (Hauptman 1981, 107). Over a century after Lewis Henry Morgan addressed Seneca concerns about treaties and land claims, and thirty years after his initial fieldwork, Fenton would testify before Congress on behalf of the Senecas over Kinzua Dam (Senate 1964, 109–11; House 1964, 504–8; Diamond, Sturtevant, and Fenton 1964, 631–33).

Life on the Allegany Reservation was peaceful and focused on villages along the river. Although Senecas had been wage laborers since before the turn of the century, primarily in logging and railroading, by the late 1950s they were dependent on wage employment (Abler and Tooker 1978, 514). In 1961 wages constituted over half of the total cash income of two-thirds (n=83) of the Seneca households in the take area for Kinzua Dam. Cash income per household ranged from less than five hundred dollars to twelve thousand dollars annually (Fuhriman 1963, 17). Only 5 of the 124 households within the take area received public assistance during the first eleven months of fiscal year 1962 (18).

The results of a survey by the BIA conducted in June 1962 indicate that households were almost equally divided between church attenders and nonattenders. Forty-three percent of the respondents indicated an active interest in the Longhouse religion of Handsome Lake (Fuhriman 1963, 31). It would appear that these beliefs had taken on a political/cultural importance even for those who professed Christianity as their religion (A. Wallace 1969, 336; *New York Times*, 10 June 1962, 59).

The most important event of the 1960s for the Seneca Nation was the construction of the Kinzua Dam in Pennsylvania. Although the political procedures involved in building the dam have been documented by Roy Brant (1970) and Laurence Hauptman (1986a), there has been no analysis of the sociocultural effects on the Seneca Nation, and particularly on the people of the Allegany Reservation who were forced to relocate. The need for such a study was recognized by George Heron, president of the Seneca Nation, in testimony before the Senate Subcommittee on Indian Affairs (Senate 1964, 85) and confirmed by Michelle Dean Stock, a Seneca teacher, relocatee, and former education director for the Seneca Nation (Dean 1983).

The dislocation suffered by the Allegany Senecas in the 1960s differed significantly from previous Seneca movements because it took place within the context of postwar U.S. industrial expansion and reflected the needs of a capitalist society in which Indians represented a distinct, though often overlooked, minority. For this reason it can be usefully compared to other forced relocations using the framework proposed by Scudder and Colson (1982).

TWO

Involuntary Relocations: An Overview

Movement from one location to another has always been a fact of human life, beginning with the seasonally cyclic wanderings of early hunter-gatherer populations. Prehistorically, the Senecas relocated their villages every twelve to twenty years as nearby woodlands became exhausted and soil fertility decreased (Richter 1992, 23). Such changes were made after a general consensus had been reached and required the construction of new longhouses and the creation of new agricultural fields. This entailed a significant amount of labor for both men and women and caused some disruption, but the benefits of increased food production, more readily available firewood, and improved hunting were readily apparent within a short time. In this case, the primary impact of removal was physical rather than emotional.

More drastic change came as a result of warfare and European invasion as the Senecas sought to remain out of harm's way within their traditional territory. In these situations, not only was movement more hurried and relocation sites less than ideal, but there was significant emotional impact as the Indians tried to cope with the loss of both lives and lands. By the end of the eighteenth century, the Senecas were restricted to a small fraction of the lands over which they had once held dominion and were struggling to survive in what was an increasingly complex world. Gender roles had changed greatly, and traditional religion no longer provided solace and solutions to Seneca problems. Reduced in size and importance, the Senecas looked to the promises of Timothy Pickering and George Washington to guarantee their remaining territory.

As the United States became more powerful militarily and economically, once again the demand for Seneca lands was heard, this time in the guise of industrial development masquerading as flood control. This assault on the land base is best understood in the context of forced removals of minority, often indigenous, populations that have occurred on all continents within the past century.

With the rise of state-level societies, and particularly of industrialism, the relatively permanent movement of human populations has taken another, less benign, aspect as people are coerced physically or psychologically to find new places to live. The World Bank estimates that between eighty and ninety million people have been resettled between 1984 and 1994 as the direct result of infrastructure programs for dams and urban development (Cernea and Guggenheim 1994, i). *Migration, resettlement, relocation, dislocation,* and *removal* are all terms found in the scientific literature to describe this phenomenon. Terminological confusion would seem to result from two factors: the specific situational determinants of the movement and the fact that this subject has only recently become a major focus of research although it is rapidly expanding. In 1976 the American Anthropological Association held a symposium titled Involuntary Migration and Resettlement: The Problems and Responses of Dislocated Peoples, and in 1988 the International Congress of Anthropological and Ethnological Sciences held a workshop on involuntary resettlement to discuss a draft of the World Bank's technical paper on the subject. In 1990 Involuntary Migration and Resettlement became a formal program at the University of Florida, and the World Bank became the first international development agency to require specific attention to the human problems involved in resettlement as a prerequisite to receiving aid (World Bank 1990).

The social engineers and politicians often responsible for involuntary movement usually see it as a necessary temporary inconvenience for the people involved, with negative effects, if any, lasting no longer than a generation. For many of these individuals, relocation is associated with the economic rewards of a job promotion and enhanced social status, and therefore the immediate negative effects (sale and purchase of home, leaving friends and co-workers, etc.) are easily outweighed by the positive ones foreseen in the not-too-distant future. The decision, therefore, to relocate people or communities is a relatively easy one, since the possibility that others might not place the same value on mobility rarely occurs to them.

A classic example of this is the statement of former secretary of state John Foster Dulles to an audience at the American University of Beirut in 1954 that the Palestinian "problem" (read Palestinian refugees) would solve itself when the new generation raised in exile moved into positions of power and forgot about Palestine (Gilmour 1980, 83). Dulles viewed the refugee problem as one of relocation, a minor, passing inconvenience, to be tolerated, alleviated if possible, but inconsequential in the long term. The tragic effects of this erroneous and inadequate assumption are readily apparent as a second generation born and raised in the camps reaches adulthood.

Sociologists analyzing relocations resulting from urban renewal programs in Boston (Fried 1963), Washington (Thursz 1973), and Buffalo (Mithun 1975) recognized that many relocatees found their distress at relocation neither minor nor temporary, and that the trauma was psychological as well as physical. This tacit recognition of relocation as a process with potential long-term negative effects was confirmed by Scudder and Colson (1972, 1979), in their joint study of the Kariba Dam Project in Zambia, and placed within a processual framework (1982). In cases such as these, where the population at risk was either not consulted or not consenting, the term *dislocation*, with its connotation of multifaceted disruption, seems more appropriate than the relatively benign *relocation*. For this reason *dislocation* is used as most descriptive of the Seneca experience; *removal*, the preferred Seneca term, will be used as a synonym.

The remainder of this chapter is devoted to a summary of the effects of some recent dislocations, examination of the model proposed by Scudder and Colson, and the history of American Indian dislocations.

EFFECTS OF OTHER RECENT DISLOCATIONS

A taxonomy of dislocation based on causative agent is useful. This provides two major categories, dislocations due to natural disaster (earthquake, flood, tornado, epidemic, etc.) and those due to human action. The latter can be subdivided into the results of war (expulsion, refuge seeking) and administrative action, either to benefit the population removed (some urban renewal projects) or for the benefit of the larger society (most development projects, particularly hydroelectric projects).

The roots of the Scudder and Colson model to be tested here actually lie in work done by William Fenton, the leading Iroquoianist scholar, and his colleague Anthony F. C. Wallace, an ethnohistorian, in a totally different context. These parallels were recognized by Fenton (1985a) himself following a presentation by Bilharz (Kolb 1985) of some of the Seneca data within the context of the Scudder and Colson model.

Anthony Wallace's (1956b) study of the Worcester, Massachusetts, tornado was an attempt to generate a model of disaster as a type of event, evaluating the responses and reactions of the victims and would-be rescuers alike. He noted that the initial response in the disaster syndrome was apathy, lasting either minutes or hours, with the length often dependent upon the extent of injury (109). Traumatized individuals compared their situation to an end-of-the-world scenario as they reacted to the destruction of their community (62). Individuals with previous leadership experience tended to lead in the immediate postdisaster period, he suggested (66), because they required less orientation to their new roles. Additionally, these individuals were frequently trained members of helping professions (clergy, medicine, fire and social control) whose community roles often came to the fore in times of crisis (64). A similar response pattern can be seen among the survivors of Hiroshima reported by John Hersey (1946).

The second phase, lasting days, was marked by a concern for the survival of the community, with personal losses minimized (A. Wallace 1956b, 109). Outsiders, particularly those in uniforms, seemed to be a stimulus for increased community action (79). The third phase was marked by enthusiastic, even euphoric, participation in the rehabilitation (109–10). Importantly, he notes (107) that even a moderately successful rehabilitation often focused on the recreation of the old, predisaster culture, an essentially conservative

response. The final phase showed a return to "normally ambivalent" attitudes, criticisms, and annoyance at long-term effects (110).

Kai Erikson's (1976) study of the 1972 Buffalo Creek flood in West
Virginia confirmed many of Wallace's hypotheses, although he
noted that the Buffalo Creek victims reacted with reflexes dulled by
the chronic catastrophe of Appalachian poverty (132). The euphoria
described by Wallace was not observed by Erikson, perhaps because
the extent of the disaster was so much greater. At Worcester, rescue
efforts came from undamaged sections of the city so that survivors
were aware that the larger community continued. Aid at Buffalo
Creek came from unknown outsiders (201), and the destruction of
the community seemed, and was, more complete. *Community* as
used here has both territorial and social meaning, although it was
the loss of the latter that was most traumatic (187). Erikson noted
(31, 41, 135, 236) that the trauma suffered by children was demonstrated by their drawings and their fear of storms, a fear shared by
many adults. The responses of children to disaster are rarely reported even in summary fashion, yet they are critical in any processual study of dislocation, as their recollections and interpreta-
tions will have direct impact on their actions as adults, a fact noted
in another context by Robert Coles (1986). Although there are no reports of the responses of Seneca children at the time they were removed, their retrospective analyses confirm the impact this event
had on their lives.

Most dislocated people are of low income and status with minimal political and economic power, so governments usually assume
they can be removed with impunity (Scudder and Colson 1982, 268).
This is true in the majority of cases, and removal is usually carried
out, although publicity and protest may force significant modifica-
tion in the government's plans or stated intentions or may result in
its embarrassment. Examples of governments being forced to can-
cel plans for removal are extremely rare, perhaps because the disori-
entation and apathy described by Wallace and Erikson function to
inhibit any concerted response to the threat. The relative power of
each group is also significant since even if a group is well organized,
the strength of the bureaucracy arrayed against the relocatees may
be intimidating and overwhelming. Yet the survivors of the earthquake that destroyed the provincial capital of Yungay, Peru, in May

1970 were able to accomplish what others had been unable to do. Today a rebuilt Yungay remains beneath the huge avalanche scar, a constant reminder of the destruction of the former village, despite all government attempts to force the citizens to move to a safer location.

Because of the severity and extent of the disaster—seventy thousand killed, a half million homeless, 152 cities and towns destroyed— aid did not reach Yungay until four days after the quake and avalanche (Oliver-Smith 1986, 11). By this time attitudes of resentment and bitterness toward an apparently uncaring government had begun to form, and the survivors had, on their own, begun to reconstruct their lives (82–83). Although aid later arrived from around the world, some useful and some irrelevant, the initial isolation may have permitted those who were still alive to create bonds among previously disparate groups, such as peasants and provincial elites, which allowed a united front against Peruvian plans to relocate the capital to Tingua, a safer location fifteen kilometers (nine miles) to the south (113).

The other successful attempt to halt dislocation is somewhat different in that the decision against removal probably had less to do with humanitarian goals or response to the plight of the people involved than with economic and political concerns. The Fort McDowell Yavapai had been removed at least five times since 1867 when, in 1947, plans for the Orme Dam in the Central Arizona Project called for the inundation of two-thirds of their land, including all of the agricultural and grazing land (Khera and Mariella 1982, 170). In 1977, despite testimony from an anthropologist that the Yavapai could survive another move, President Jimmy Carter canceled the Central Arizona Project. He later rescinded this order only under the condition that the Orme Dam be deleted from the project (172, 175), thus sparing the Yavapai another dislocation.

More data are available on administrative removals because, unlike natural disasters, they require some level of pre-removal study or action. Additionally, they occur within centralized political systems, thereby generating considerable documentation of the bureaucratic perspective. The smallest category of administrative removals is that designed to benefit the dislocated population. Examples of this type include the evacuation of pro–United States

Vietnamese after the fall of Saigon in 1975, the relocation of the Hausa to limit their exposure to sleeping sickness, slum eradication in Cuba after the 1959 revolution, and the evacuation plans for American cities prior to the outbreak of nuclear hostilities.

The experience of Vietnamese refugees is instructive because it runs counter to the stereotype of refugees as poverty-stricken, uneducated, possibly starving people fleeing war, famine, or political repression with nothing other than the clothes on their backs and grateful for the most meager attention. To the surprise of American officials, many of the deplaning Vietnamese in Guam were well dressed and carrying golf clubs and tennis racquets (Morrison and Moos 1982, 53) and were somewhat taken aback by the spartan accommodations that had been arranged within only two hours of the receipt of the order at the American military base (50). Another difference between the Vietnamese and others in this category was their agreement on the necessity of removal, as they feared for their lives under a communist regime due to their previous association with the Americans. Because of the crisis conditions under which evacuation occurred and the numbers of people involved, the military actually carried out the operation, although the State Department was nominally in charge (55). In fact, Morrison and Moos (65) argue that in any emergency mass removal only the military (at least in the United States) has the requisite experience, organization, and matériel to cope with the situation.

The Vietnamese experience on Guam is instructive in other ways as well. Despite the wide spectrum of education, age, social status, and wealth, they were still refugees whose plans, ultimate destination, and political status were unknown; in the words of the commander of naval forces in the Marianas, they were people "halfway to nowhere" (Morrison and Moos 1982, 49). Status differences among dislocated peoples have rarely been considered, primarily since those groups closely studied have been relatively homogeneous, yet the Vietnamese example indicates that the psychological trauma undergone by rich and poor alike was significant and suggests that higher-status individuals may be even more deeply affected since they may suffer a severe decrease in status in addition to physical and economic deprivation.

The majority of Vietnamese who resettled permanently in the United States after the fall of Saigon were middle or upper-middle class, and approximately half of the young people were bilingual (Pisarowicz and Tosher 1982, 72). Of the 133,133 Vietnamese who entered the United States between April and December 1975, about 15,000 settled in the Denver metropolitan area (71–72). By 1977 a Vietnamese community, Sun Valley, had formed in a Denver public housing development, which attracted Vietnamese refugees from many places in the country (74). Those who settled in Sun Valley differed significantly from those who settled in noncommunity settings. To a great extent this reflected differences in pre-removal circumstances. Sun Valley Vietnamese tended to be less professional (often they had been laborers and rural residents), had poorer English language skills, and thus faced more serious difficulties in finding and maintaining employment (75). Settlement within a Vietnamese community was therefore an essentially conservative strategy, an attempt to maintain a rural pattern. Membership within the community probably aided in defining positive self-images, but Pisarowicz and Tosher suggest it may have hindered short-term adaptation since members were able to use the community as a "crutch" (79). Nevertheless, community Vietnamese seemed happier overall than their noncommunity compatriots, who expressed a greater desire to return to Vietnam, perhaps because their relative deprivation vis-à-vis non-Vietnamese was more apparent and accentuated feelings of acute status loss (76–77).

Administrative removals may work best in situations in which there is at least partial agreement on the cause for dislocation. In 1937 the British government instituted the Anchau Scheme in Nigeria in an attempt to meet the increased problem of sleeping sickness. While the Hausa, who were primarily afflicted by the disease, recognized the relationship between the tse-tse fly and the shaded stream bank environment, they did not accept a connection between the environment and the disease (Miner 1960, 164–65). When the government decided to keep stream banks clear, thus forcing the resettlement of some Hausa villages, the specific methods of implementation were left up to native authorities in order to minimize disruption. The Hausa feared sleeping sickness and in the past had relocated when epidemics threatened (166), thus the government directive, while not fully understood, was not greeted with the degree of skepticism or resistance that would be expected had it been imposed by totally unknown authorities for completely alien reasons.

A significant amount of stress is incurred even by members of communities that actively seek relocation. The process leading to the resettlement of the island of St. Kilda off the western coast of Scotland began in the late nineteenth century when most children expressed the desire to leave the island as adults. New housing, requiring foreign materials and maintenance methods, created unsatisfied needs and greater reliance on charity (Maclean 1972, 129). In August 1930 the entire community was evacuated following a petition signed by all adults to the British secretary of state requesting such action. It is interesting that they did not request to be relocated as a community, although most went to live in the same area (141). Despite the fact that nearly everyone, except a few elders who wished to die on St. Kilda, desired the move, many elders and middle-aged individuals died shortly after arrival on the mainland. Younger people experienced fewer problems, as did those who settled in rural rather than urban environs (143).

Elimination of slum housing is usually perceived as benefiting the former slum dwellers. This is belied by the fact that in the United States ten times as many low-income housing units have been destroyed as have been built (Robertson 1981, 554), the ultimate beneficiaries being members of the upper-middle class. Underlying the obvious poverty in materially substandard areas are often strong bonds of community whose disruption brings feelings of grief that can be seen in frequent symptoms of physical, social, and psychological distress, depression, anger, and nostalgia. In addition, there is a tendency to idealize the former location (Fried 1963, 151). Although some people were happy with the removal, Fried noted that 46 percent of the individuals dislocated from an urban slum in Boston's West End reported a fairly severe grief reaction (152). The longer an individual identified with the geographic and social community, the greater chance there was of a severe grief reaction (155). Fried suggests that either spatial or group identity may be the focus of continuity, and that if both of these are localized in the same residential area, disruption is much greater (158). In order to cope with this disruption, some families try to relocate as close to their previous home as possible, maintaining some semblance of spatial orientation, or move in among relatives, thus accentuating the group or family orientation (160).

Responses to dislocation are independent of political system, as shown by Douglas Butterworth's (1980) study of Buena Ventura, a low-income housing project constructed in post-revolutionary Cuba. The initial response of the residents of the Las Yaguas slum when told they would be removed to the new settlement of Buena Ventura was that this was just another in a series of attempts to evict them without compensation. In fact, shortly after the revolution Castro was concerned about substandard housing and wanted to relocate slum dwellers to modern, multiple-dwelling buildings in middle-class neighborhoods (18, 20). Only when resettlement was under way did the people actually realize the government was serious.

Buena Ventura, like nearly all relocation areas, was the product of middle-class planners whose concern with superficial disorder and material poverty led them to completely miss the underlying sense of community, spatial arrangements (particularly privacy), and camaraderie that marked Las Yaguas (Butterworth 1980, 65). Despite the influx of social workers genuinely concerned with the welfare of the people, improvements in material well-being were not accompanied by an enhanced quality of life. There was less visiting, the sense of community was lost, nostalgia was widespread, and some even stated a preference for Las Yaguas (68–69).

During World War II, William Fenton, the acknowledged dean of Iroquoian studies, was secretary of the Smithsonian Institution's War Committee. In this capacity he served on various National Research Council committees providing anthropological and psychological advice to federal agencies. In 1951 he was appointed executive secretary to the Division of Anthropology and Psychology in the National Research Council and held this position until 1954, when he was appointed assistant commissioner of the New York State Museum and Science Center in Albany. While in Washington, he was involved with the National Security Council and the Civil Defense Administration in considering the relative merits of shelter construction versus evacuation as a protection against nuclear warfare (A. Wallace 1984, 3). Among the disaster researchers Fenton recruited was Anthony F. C. Wallace, whose study of the 1953 Worcester tornado (1956b) was published by the Committee on Disaster Studies of the National Research Council.

Although the early disaster studies appear to have been prompted by concern over nuclear warfare, it is ironic that their results seem to have been ignored by the Federal Emergency Management Agency (FEMA), successor to the Civil Defense Administration and the Civil Defense Preparedness Agency. Despite increased evidence to the contrary, a 1972 report by Dynes, Quarantelli, and Kreps entitled "A Perspective on Disaster Planning" states that "the 'disaster syndrome' does not appear in great numbers of people; seems confined only to the most sudden traumatic kinds of disasters; has been reported only in certain cultural settings; and is generally of short duration, hours only, if not minutes" (cited in Lifton, Markusen, and Austin 1984, 287). Therefore, FEMA argues that the population in high-risk urban areas can realistically be evacuated in 3.3 days (Brand 1984, 82) and assumes that the millions of relocatees will receive a warm reception from their rural "hosts," who will openly share with them needed skills and resources (Lipsky 1984, 156). This assumption seems to be based on analogies with natural disasters where heightened community spirit may be noted in the early stages. This analogy would seem far-fetched at best since the time period involved in relocation, particularly if war occurs, is unspecified and the availability of outside aid unlikely.

THE SCUDDER-COLSON MODEL

Thayer Scudder and Elisabeth Colson proposed the first model for the study of dislocation. They stated that individuals and the sociocultural system respond to dislocation in predictable ways because the stress of forced removal limits the range of coping responses (1982, 267). This stress occurs on three levels: physiological, psychological, and sociocultural.

Physiological stress is reflected in increased rates of morbidity and mortality (Scudder and Colson 1982, 269). In many cases this is difficult to document since adequate demographic statistics are often unavailable, especially for rural ethnic minorities. Informants often report increased numbers of deaths among the elderly occurring within the first few years of removal. While much of this data necessarily remains anecdotal, there is increasing documentation (Fahim 1983, 73; Scudder and Colson 1982, 112; Heller 1982) that increased mortality does result from forced removal, although Borup, Gallego, and Heffernan found no correlation between the movement of elderly nursing home residents and increased mortality (1979, 137). Where appropriate data are available, attention should focus upon the cause of death as well as the age cohort. Because the quality and quantity of health care may decline precipitously during the time of removal, the very old and very young may be at greatest risk. However, Shkilnyk (1985, 12, 13) has noted a massive increase in death rates among teenagers and young adults following the dislocation from Grassy Narrows, an Ojibwa community in Ontario. Suicides accounted for 35 percent of all deaths in the fifteen to twenty-one age cohort (235) and were often alcohol related. There were also many unsuccessful suicide attempts. Increased rates of substance abuse have been noted by Shkilnyk (18–25) and Anthony Oliver-Smith (1986, 103) among others, and while this has usually been cited as an example of psychological stress, its relationship to increased mortality warrants further exploration. A more recent example of this would be the community at Davis Inlet, Labrador, where 25 percent of the adult population attempted suicide in 1992 and more than one in nine youths are chronic gas sniffers.

Psychological stress has four components, not all of which need be operative in each person (Scudder and Colson 1982, 269–70). Trauma is most likely to occur among people forced to leave their homes abruptly. Perlman (1982, 233) states that *favela* residents in Brazil might receive only twenty-four hours notice of their removal. A similar pattern occurred in South African removals of "surplus people" (Platzky and Walker 1986, 133). Guilt also occurs most often when removal has been abrupt. Survivors of natural disasters often have a hard time understanding why they, rather than their child, spouse, or other loved one, were spared (Oliver-Smith 1986, 101–2; Lifton 1967, 489).

The final components of psychological stress are grief, especially for the lost home and community (Fried 1963), and anxiety (Scudder and Colson 1982, 270). Dislocated peoples stressed by removal are unsure of what the future holds, and sometimes are even ignorant of where the future will be.

Sociocultural stress refers to the political, economic, and other cultural effects of dislocation (Scudder and Colson 1982, 270–71). A leadership vacuum frequently results as the previous leaders may be discredited or dispersed. Failure to successfully oppose removal can lead to loss of status from within the threatened community. On the other hand, strong action against dislocation can result in political action being taken by government authorities to remove recalcitrant local leaders. There may also be a major reduction in the cultural inventory due to a loss (temporary or permanent) of behavioral patterns, economic practices, symbols, or institutions.

The nature and extent of these stresses influence peoples' coping strategies both during and after dislocation. These strategies are basically conservative (Scudder and Colson 1982, 271), sometimes leading the threatened community to deny that removal will occur, even when confronted with overwhelming evidence to the contrary (Colson 1971, 41). This rejection of the idea of removal may indicate that it is simply too stressful to acknowledge (Scudder and Colson 1982, 271), or it may reflect a series of threatened removals never effected and therefore be a logical response.

The process of relocation was originally described as occurring in four stages (Scudder and Colson 1982, 274–75), but the model was expanded to five stages by Scudder (1993), who subdivided the first stage into two by separating government planning from the initial infrastructure development in the relocation sites. Scudder himself was not convinced that the expanded framework would be useful (130) and later returned to a four-stage model (1997). The following discussion uses the most recent version and its terminology.

The initial Planning and Recruitment stage occurs when government policymakers decide that a given population will be removed. At this time the sites of resettlement (if they are to be provided) are determined. Careful consideration of the sociocultural characteristics of the population is necessary at this stage since decisions now will determine the length and severity of the following stages and may preclude the occurrence of the third stage. These plans are frequently made without any consultation with the people at risk. The length of this stage can be measured in years or generations. Once a government has decided on removal, investment in the area to be impacted is reduced or eliminated and the inhabitants may experience the beginning of a decline in their standard of living even though they are unaware of its cause. This stage ends with the relocation of the people to the new site, which frequently lacks an adequate infrastructure.

The second stage, Adjustment and Coping, is a time of multidimensional stress as people try to adjust to their new surroundings. Responses are conservative as they cling to familiar routines as much as possible and rely on kin and co-ethnics. This stage lasts a minimum of two years (Scudder 1997, 682; Scudder and Colson 1982, 280). Local leadership is often undermined or coopted. Palestinian refugees are clearly still in this stage fifty years after fleeing their homes (Gilmour 1980; Sayigh 1979), although they may represent an extreme example. Toward the end of this stage, some households break out of a conservative stance and develop social and economic ties to a broader community, thereby increasing their risk taking.

The groups that move into the third stage, Economic Development and Community Formation, reflect increasingly open-ended societies in which there is a rise in initiative and risk taking in the majority of households. An increase in standards of living and widening wealth differentials become apparent. This stage is never reached in many dislocations because the settlements fail and people relocate themselves elsewhere. Without population dispersion, people can remain in the third stage if they are dependent on outside aid and are unwilling to risk what little they have (Scudder and Colson 1982, 275). Major indications that this stage has been reached include "feeling at home" (familiarity with the landscape and new subsistence patterns), the undertaking of new economic pursuits, and the emergence of effective local leadership that interacts with the larger sociopolitical sphere (280–81). A willingness to invest in education seems common in societies that reach this stage, although its roots may lie in the previous one (281). Non-kin-based organizations may also begin in the second stage, often dealing with life crises, but appear more fully developed in this stage. The evolution of these organizations into more powerful political units, if it occurs, is unclear (282).

The increasingly dynamic investment strategies and cultural renaissance typical of stage three must be institutionally, economically, and environmentally sustainable for a relocation to be considered successful (Scudder 1997, 683). The final stage, Incorporation and Handing Over, is analogous to Anthony Wallace's (1956a) consolidation stage in a revitalization movement. The process ends when political and economic leadership shifts to a second generation that identifies with the new community. Outside aid from government or charitable agencies is phased out, and responsibility for these programs is taken by the local government. Additionally, the community is incorporated into a larger territorial framework, including surrounding cities and towns, and regional and national economic, commercial, and political networks. The processes included within this stage have not been researched (Scudder and Colson 1982, 275; Scudder 1993, 134).

AMERICAN INDIAN RELOCATIONS

The Seneca removal must also be seen within the context of European and American policies toward Indians. The dislocation of indigenous North American populations began at contact, although their resettlement west of the Mississippi did not become the avowed policy of the U.S. government until the passage of the 1830 Removal Bill. By that time most of the eastern Indians fit into the Scudder and Colson model of dislocated peoples as politically weak minorities. The only possible exceptions to this were the "Five Civilized Tribes" of the Southeast whose removal along the Trail of Tears to Oklahoma was the first major government-sponsored dislocation of native peoples. The tragic effects of these removals have been well documented (Foreman 1934, 1946, 1953; Green 1982; Satz 1975; A. Wallace 1993; Wardell 1977; Washburn 1971).

Another major attempt at Indian relocation, this time as individuals to urban centers, began in the 1950s as a response to postwar reservation crowding and high unemployment (Madigan 1956, 3), especially among the Navajos (Fixico 1986, 135). At the same time, the Eisenhower administration witnessed an increase in transfer of land from Indians to non-Indians. In the fiscal year that ended 30 June 1954, a half million acres (3,200 tracts representing 3.5 percent of all acreage held by Indian individuals) were removed from trust or restricted status. There were 1,609 sales to non-Indians; 88 tracts were purchased from non-Indians for Indian tribes or individuals (Washburn 1971, 147). By the end of 1954, 6,200 Indians had resettled in large cities (Fixico 1986, 138).

Although urban relocation is usually associated with the Eisenhower presidency, its roots are actually in the Truman administration. In 1950 Truman fired Bureau of Indian Affairs commissioner John Nichols and replaced him with Dillon S. Myer, who had previously headed the War Relocation Authority (Fixico 1986, 63). Myer was a strong believer in Indian assimilation and favored the dissolution of the BIA as soon as possible. To this end he urged a program of job training and placement assistance for Indians wishing to leave the reservation as well as aid to reservations in order to attract industrial development (66–67).

The Voluntary Relocation Program formally began in 1952 under the auspices of the Bureau of Indian Affairs. Its goal was to provide financial aid and some social services to Indian individuals and families who desired to permanently relocate from reservations (Madigan 1956, 3; Fixico 1986, 136). Cities were chosen as relocation sites on the basis of diversified industrial employment opportunities. Relocation offices were opened in Los Angeles in 1951, Chicago and Denver in 1952, Oakland in 1954, San Francisco in 1955, and San Jose and St. Louis in 1956 (Madigan 1956, 5). Duties of the reservation relocation officer included publication of relocation and employment opportunities and living conditions in the appropriate cities and processing of applications for relocation. An individual relocation plan was to be developed by the individual or family in consultation with the reservation relocation officer once the applicant(s) had been accepted. A copy of this plan was then to be forwarded to the relocation office in the chosen city. Once the application was approved, the reservation relocation officer was to aid the relocatee in planning his or her move (6). Besides working with individual applicants, reservation relocation officers were to work closely with tribal governments to explain the program and with the relevant state agencies to ensure that Indians were able to fully utilize their services. City relocation officers were to develop employment opportunities for Indians and promote their acceptance into the community, working with labor unions, housing authorities, and religious and welfare agencies (7).

Upon arrival in the relocation city, the relocatee or the relocated family were to be met at the terminal transportation point if requested or to report as soon as possible to the relocation office, where temporary housing would be arranged and employment counseling would begin. Once the relocatee found employment, he or she would be aided in the search for a permanent home and receive information on the available community social and recreational services. Social services, including counseling, home visits, and education assistance, would be available from the relocation office during the period of adjustment, but it was assumed that by the end of a year the relocatee would be self-sufficient, and services could only be continued beyond that time under special circumstances. Those relocatees who needed it could receive financial aid for transportation to the city, movement of household goods, subsistence en route and prior to employment, and tools and equipment needed in apprenticeship programs (Madigan 1956, 7).

Despite the cooperative framework within which relocation was approached, some overeager relocation officers "encouraged" urban migration by painting an unrealistic image of Indian life in the cities in order to fill an actual or perceived quota for relocatees (Fixico 1986, 153). Relocated urban Indians soon became the focal point for social science research (Ablon 1964; Brinker and Tailor 1974; Chadwick and Stauss 1975; Graves 1971; Graves and Van Arsdale 1966; Hurt 1961; Martin 1964; Price 1968; Snyder 1971; Weppner 1971). Most reported a high percentage of returnees to the reservations, as many as 75 percent in the early years of the program (Ablon 1964, 297), although the BIA reported only a 30 percent return rate for the years 1953–57 (Fixico 1986, 149). Navajos returning from Los Angeles cited social and emotional reasons, such as illness or alcoholism, as the primary reasons (Price 1968, 171). A similar pattern was noted by Graves and Van Arsdale (1966, 302) for Navajos leaving Denver. More recent studies of urban Indians (Guillemin 1975;

Krotz 1980; Sorkin 1978) have cited high levels of drunkenness and anti-social behavior within these groups of voluntary relocatees.

During World War II, twenty-five thousand Indians served in the U.S. military, 90 percent of whom were enlisted men. The overwhelming majority (twenty-two thousand) saw duty in the army on the front lines (Fixico 1986, 4, 7). In addition, nearly three hundred Indian women joined the nurses' corps, military auxiliaries, or the Red Cross, and fifty thousand Indians worked in war industries (5–6). For many non-Indians, particularly in government, this was clear evidence that Indians could, and therefore should, be assimilated into mainstream American life and Indian services terminated. That Indians might not find assimilation desirable was not considered by government planners despite evidence to the contrary, such as the founding, in 1944, of the National Congress of American Indians (NCAI) as a response to the threat of termination (22). By the 1950s, termination and relocation had become the major goals of federal Indian policy (135).

Fixico (1986, 147) states that veterans had the easiest time adjusting to urban life, probably because of previous experience with non-Indians. Many veterans did relocate to cities (approximately one-third of the Indian relocatees in Ablon's (1964) San Francisco study were veterans), but Martin (1964, 290, 293) states that while experience in the military was a factor contributing to the decision to migrate to the city, what was learned during that experience was more important than the experience itself.

Relocation of Canadian indigenous peoples also became more common at this time, prompted by a government mandate to improve native reserves, with an emphasis on housing and education. Justification for these removals was often based on technical or logistical imperatives. For example, in 1963 the Department of Indian Affairs and Northern Development (DIAND) relocated the people of Grassy Narrows, an Ojibwa reserve in Ontario located twelve hundred miles northwest of Toronto, five miles to the south because it claimed a road could not be built to the old reserve on the islands and peninsulas of the English-Wabigoon River—despite the fact that a logging road already existed from Kenora to Grassy Narrows (Shkilnyk 1985, 169). In the concluding chapter we return to the

Grassy Narrows experience because it stands in stark contrast to the contemporary removal at Allegany.

The postwar decades, with the attendant Cold War and growing economy, witnessed the expansion of large-scale development projects, especially large dams to generate electricity and for flood control. Because tribal groups traditionally lived in river valleys, they were particularly disrupted by these projects.

The Pick-Sloan Plan had the most widespread and severe effects on Indian populations. The primary beneficiaries of this plan to control flooding along the Missouri River were white farmers. Because the actions of the Army Corps of Engineers and the responses of the Sioux people involved are directly tied to congressional actions on the Kinzua Dam, they are examined in some detail.

The Pick-Sloan Plan, a joint water development program of the Army Corps of Engineers and the Bureau of Reclamation, began in 1944 and "caused more damage to Indian land than any other public works project in America" (Lawson 1982, xxi). The affected tribes included Chippewa, Mandan, Hidatsa, Arikara, Shoshone, Arapaho, Crow, Cree, Blackfoot, Assiniboine, and every group with land along the Missouri or its tributaries (xxi). The project led to the construction of four dams—Garrison, Fort Randall, Oahe, Big Bend—which resulted in the inundation of 550 square miles of tribal lands in North and South Dakota and the dislocation of over nine hundred Indian families. These dams reduced the land base of five Sioux reservations by approximately 6 percent, forced a third of the population to relocate, and reduced the wild game and plant supply by 75 percent (55–56). Most of the damage was incurred on Sioux land on the Standing Rock, Cheyenne River, Lower Brule, Crow Creek, and Yankton Reservations in the Dakotas, but the most devastating effects on a single reservation were felt by the Three Affiliated Tribes (Mandan, Hidatsa, Arikara) of the Fort Berthold Reserve in North Dakota, whose tribal life was almost completely destroyed by the Garrison Dam (27–28).

Despite treaty rights that provided for tribal consent to land exchange, the tribes were not consulted, and the Sioux knew little about the Pick-Sloan Plan until long after its approval. Although the BIA was aware of the plan, it voiced no objections during the 1944 congressional debate. Tribal water rights under the Winters

Doctrine were ignored, and dam construction on reservation land began prior to the opening of any formal negotiations with the tribes.

Changes resulting from dislocation were most apparent in the economic sphere. The livestock industry was crippled on all but the Yankton Reservation by the flooding of bottomland grazing areas. Irrigation was almost impossible because the dams inundated most of the potentially irrigable land. Because the new houses could not be heated by wood stoves, new sources for fuel, food, water, and lumber were required. The economy changed from one based on subsistence to one based on cash, and there was disorganization in the social, political, and religious spheres as well, resulting in anxiety, resentment, and insecurity (Lawson 1982, 57–58). It should be noted, however, that the Pick-Sloan Plan was originally welcomed by many tribal leaders, including the Crow Creek Tribal Council, which unanimously favored the plan in a vote in May 1947, a vote that the BIA agency superintendent advised it to reconsider (58–59).

The Garrison Dam made members of the Three Affiliated Tribes on the Fort Berthold Reserve in North Dakota the first to deal with the Army Corps when it entered the reservation without warning to begin construction. The Sioux filed legal action based on the 1851 Fort Laramie Treaty, and Congress halted expenditures for the dam until a suitable settlement was made with the Indians. Had they not appealed to Congress, the only monetary settlement that the Sioux would have received would have been based on corps appraisals subject to court appeals, the procedure established for other lands needed for public works (Lawson 1982, 59–62).

Construction of the Fort Randall Dam began a month after that of the Garrison Dam. Violating the Yankton Treaty of 1858, the Army Corps condemned the parcels it needed (3,349 acres of Yankton Sioux land) without consulting either the tribe or the BIA. The violation went unchallenged by either, although the BIA later "haggled" with the corps over the adequacy of appraisals and asked Congress for eight-five thousand dollars for relocation sites, which was received six years after removal (Lawson 1982, 63–64).

In order to avoid similar problems with the Oahe Dam, Acting Indian Commissioner William Zimmerman asked General Lewis Pick of the Missouri Basin division of the corps not to condemn Indian land but instead to cooperate with the BIA in establishing a more humane procedure. Congress also enacted legislation in September 1959 making the army chief of engineers and the secretary of the interior responsible for negotiating settlements, which tribal members could appeal in federal court at army expense. It also required payment not only for Indian land and improvements but also for relocation costs "so that their economic, social, religious, and community life can be re-established and protected" (Lawson 1982, 65). Although the law stated that negotiations could not interfere with construction schedules, the settlement could take effect only after it had been approved by 75 percent of the adult tribal members on each reservation as stipulated by treaty and ratified by an act of Congress (66). Ultimately the corps was unable to reach an agreement with any of the tribes. The Standing Rock Sioux sent a delegation to Washington, which camped out in Secretary Chapman's office and was supported by Harold Ickes, Gene Weltfish, Oliver LaFarge, the American Bar Association, and the Daughters of the American Revolution (71). They received their money at the last minute, but the Crow Creek and Lower Brule Sioux had to move before an agreement was reached (68).

Although the army promised the people of Standing Rock that money would be available immediately after the settlement act was passed in September 1958, the Indians got no funds until January 1959. In November the news media picked up on a report by the state welfare office that the Standing Rock Sioux were suffering because of neglect by the army; the American people responded by sending food and money, and Congress responded by increasing the tribe's annual assistance by forty-six thousand dollars. Eviction orders were issued for January 1960, when temperatures were thirty degrees below zero and no funds were available yet for new home construction or old home relocation, so the Indians were crowded into trailers that they had to maintain at their own expense. Only later did they learn the eviction date was purely arbitrary (Lawson 1982, 144–45).

Michael Lawson's primary concern was in documenting the relations of the Army Corps of Engineers and the Indians along the Missouri River and the short-term effects of removal, but many of his observations have a major bearing on the Senecas' experience. Services were curtailed during removal, and the most serious effects were on the Indian economy as previously noted. Those who had depended on wild resources for subsistence and fuel had to look elsewhere for things previously free and accessible. All of the tribes established farming and ranching programs and set aside funds for family improvement, education, and business and industrial development (Lawson 1982, 161). Improving the educational level of tribal members was often a major goal, with the Standing Rock Sioux establishing their own community college at Fort Yates, providing low-interest loans for students in college and vocational schools, and making outright grants of six hundred dollars for each year of study successfully completed (166). The Cheyenne River program experienced a high (54 percent) dropout rate in its first two years, but later 79 of 291 participants completed their education (167).

Many of the business and industrial development ideas developed by the tribes failed or did not employ significant numbers of Indians. To some extent this reflected unrealistic goals, lack of reservation resources, and lack of practical administrative experience. Internal political turmoil in several tribes led to charges of fraud and abuse, resulting in the impeachment of the Standing Rock chair in 1959 and the resignation of the Cheyenne River chair in 1962. Neither, however, was found guilty of wrongdoing in regard to the rehabilitation programs (Lawson 1982, 171). The primary complaint about the rehabilitation programs was that they were too mixed up with tribal politics (177).

The flooding of bottomlands and the reduction of wildlife led to a decrease in the recreational activities of many Indians, and attempts to attract tourists to tribal recreational developments were less than successful, often falling victim to anti-Indian economic bias. Standing Rock built a large tourist complex with a restaurant, lounge, motel, conference center, campground, golf course, indoor pool, museum, and restored Indian village. It, like a less ambitious version built by the Crow Creek Sioux at Fort Thompson, failed (Lawson 1982, 188).

Despite the rehabilitation programs that resulted from removal and the social programs of the New Frontier and the Great Society in the 1960s, unemployment at Crow Creek was 70 percent in 1971

(the lowest rate was 32 percent at Cheyenne River), and at Standing
Rock in 1972, 46 percent of the housing was substandard, 35 percent
of the homes were without electricity, and 16 percent were without
running water (Lawson 1982, 175). Nostalgia and grief were apparent. As one Cheyenne River rancher told Michael Lawson, "Like
any other Indian, . . . I'd been hard up and I was waiting for my
money, never realizing what we were losing. We look back now to
see that we lost everything . . . we had the best part of our life in that
area" (159).

By the late 1950s when plans for the construction of a dam on the
Allegheny River moved into high gear, there were a number of
trends on the national level that boded ill for the Allegany Senecas.
The long history of Indian removals in the United States meant that
many, if not most, Americans believed that there were few Indians
remaining east of the Mississippi and that the vast majority of them
were culturally indistinguishable from non-Indians. Furthermore,
federal policy toward Indians emphasized termination of the relationship between tribes and the national government based on the
assumption that the noteworthy service of Indians during World
War II proved there was no need for the continuation of governmental paternalism. The stress on homogeneity of the McCarthy era
was not in accordance with groups wishing to emphasize their
unique status. Assimilation was the order of the day.

Well-intentioned programs of urban renewal, designed by middle-class bureaucrats, were being instituted in many areas to alleviate outward signs of material poverty with little regard for the intangible social networks that would be disrupted or destroyed. A
greatly improved standard of living was believed to be within the
grasp of all Americans, even though it might initially entail some
brief inconveniences. As people moved to suburban housing developments and industry boomed, there was a concomitant increased
need for electricity; hydroelectric power seemed a reasonable
source. General Dwight Eisenhower, who had developed a close relationship with the Army Corps of Engineers, became president.
Eisenhower and the corps, which had reversed its policy against
building reservoirs (Smith 1975, 19), stood ready to receive new orders. The negative impact of the Missouri dams on Indian peoples

had little effect on the engineers but would be recalled and utilized by the Senecas and their Quaker supporters.

Meanwhile, in Pennsylvania these trends fit easily with state and local plans. As with the Allegheny and Monongahela Rivers, the point of conjunction was Pittsburgh.

THREE

Building Kinzua Dam:
Broken Treaties

The idea of a dam on the upper Allegheny River probably had its inception in 1908, when the Pittsburgh Chamber of Commerce organized the Flood Commission of Pittsburgh, which recommended a series of reservoirs to control flooding and encourage industrial growth in the city. The preeminence of industrial interests is indicated by the fact that the commission was headed by H. J. Heinz (Hauptman 1986a, 91). Seneca attempts to halt the dam began in 1927 (90), and the dam was declared economically infeasible in 1928 (Brant 1970, 13). By 1924 the Army Corps of Engineers had become actively involved, issuing a report in 1929 calling for a series of dams for power production. Ironically, the first corps engineers to survey the later dam site were ferried across the Allegheny in a johnboat by Merrill Bowen, who would later lead the Cornplanter heirs in their futile fight to save the lands given to Cornplanter by the Commonwealth of Pennsylvania. Bowen would also become an elected councilor of the Seneca Nation and serve as editor of the *Kinzua Planning Newsletter.*

In the 1930s the corps was working with special interest groups and various Pittsburgh companies to promote what would become the Kinzua Dam. A dam would benefit Pittsburgh industrialists by keeping the Allegheny River at a uniform level, thereby reducing the pollution from sulphurous drainage from the coal mines, which was rusting the boilers in the steel factories (Hauptman 1986a, 92).

Thirty years later Congressman James Haley (D-FL) would state, "this construction of the Kinzua Dam principally was to flush out the Allegheny River when it began to smell at Pittsburgh" (House 1964, 363).

Arguments against the dam were reversed in 1936 after a record-setting flood in Pittsburgh (Brant 1970, 43). The plans of Mayor David Lawrence and industrialist Richard Mellon for a Pittsburgh renaissance also required a dam. Beginning in 1936, Congress passed three flood control acts dealing with Pittsburgh and vicinity. The 1936 act included Kinzua Dam as one of a series of nine reservoirs; the dam was also included in 1938 as part of a general flood control plan for the Ohio River basin. The 1941 act contained modifications for pollution abatement and regulation of stream flow to aid navigation, but once again no funds were appropriated (Hauptman 1986a, 92–93). In the meantime, the Senecas living on the Cornplanter Grant in Pennsylvania, which would also be inundated by dam construction, appealed to anthropologists for help in stopping the dam (Cornplanter Tribe 1935).

The potential loss of this grant, the last Indian land in Pennsylvania, was noted in the *Altoona Tribune* (5 February 1940) as well as the *Williamsport Grit* (7 January 1941), both communities more than a hundred miles away. The latter included photographs of Cornplanter "Chief" Windsor Pierce and the school and church at "Indiantown." It is clear that at this time many people in Pennsylvania, including the Cornplanters, saw the construction of Kinzua Dam as a very real possibility. That power and industry rather than flood control were the driving forces behind the dam was also understood. To a letter dated 9 January 1941 to Merle Deardorff, a Warren, Pennsylvania, banker and respected amateur historian, Salamanca attorney Charles Congdon added a handwritten note: "I hear they are going to tie the Kinzua Dam to the Defense Program as a power necessity and build it right away, so that if someone drops a firecracker down the chute at Niagara they can make juice at Kinzua" (Deardorff Papers, Box 2).

The dam was stopped in the 1940s in part because Aubrey Lawrence and C. C. Daniels, who headed the Public Lands Division of the Department of Justice, opposed attempts to flood Seneca lands. Harold Ickes, secretary of the interior, also opposed the dam, reaffirming the position taken by the department in 1936. In 1940 Assistant Secretary of the Interior Oscar Chapman wrote the Department of the Army, emphasizing the federal-Seneca treaty relationship and rejecting plans for a dam. He noted that even if Seneca assent were obtained, a separate bill should be passed by Congress in recognition of the treaty relationship (Hauptman 1986a, 93).

With a change in administration in 1953, the Departments of Justice and the Interior, which had opposed the dam in the previous decades, now supported it. Laurence Hauptman (1986a) argues persuasively that the fight to stop Kinzua Dam was doomed from the time Eisenhower took office and created a special assistant for public works planning on his White House staff, which "sealed the fate of the Seneca Nation of Indians' lands" (Hauptman 1986a, 104). The man Eisenhower appointed to this position was Major General John S. Bragdon, a native of Pittsburgh, educated at Carnegie Institute, and former deputy chief of the Army Corps of Engineers. General Lucius Clay, another key presidential adviser, had served in the Pittsburgh district of the corps in the 1930s and was an early proponent of dam projects on the Allegheny (106). With such strong inside support, dam construction was nearly inevitable. Rather than operate independently, Bragdon relied increasingly on the opinions of the corps, which never doubted that the project was necessary, "portending the near incestuous relationship between his office and the federal agency in the months to come" (109).

The Seneca Nation that confronted the new dam threat was clearly no match for the federal executive. The SNI government, which met twice a year, primarily to discuss lease issues, was dominated by members of the People's Party, who tended to be owners of large parcels of land. Election was won on grounds of personality and family alliances; there were few issues, no full-time officials, no staff, and only one government building, the old courthouse. Despite their lack of training and experience, Seneca officials realized by September 1956 that the new threat was more serious than previous ones, so they sent a five-member delegation to a conference with the BIA. They were represented at this conference by the SNI attorney, Edward O'Neill, who, until 1953, had worked with Aubrey Lawrence and the Public Lands Division of the Department of Justice (Hauptman 1986a, 100).

The first formal approach to the Seneca Nation by the Army Corps of Engineers occurred in October 1956, a month before the Seneca elections. In response, the SNI Council voted to bar the corps from any surveying on Nation land. This was ignored, and in November O'Neill filed an injunction against the surveyors, Alster and Associates, requesting five thousand dollars in damages for trespassing. In the spirit of compromise that was to mark all Seneca negotiations, he offered to withdraw the suit if the surveyors agreed not to enter the reservation without the Nation's approval. November also witnessed the election of Cornelius Seneca, from Cattaraugus, as the new president. Under his leadership, the Nation began to actively seek public support for its position.

At the request of an unidentified "leading Friend," President Seneca contacted Arthur E. Morgan, former head of the Tennessee Valley Authority and longtime foe of the corps. Morgan (1971, 317) stated, "I never had worked with the American Indians, had not taken a very active interest in them, and indeed did not know of the existence of the Seneca Nation." Despite this, Morgan was instrumental in delaying construction, thereby gaining valuable time for the Senecas to rally support and organize. He and former colleague Barton Jones developed several alternative plans to the Kinzua Dam that would have spared Seneca land, but all were rejected by the corps. As Charles Congdon noted, "Flooding the Conewango Valley would provide more water for Pittsburgh, but it would flood out white folks! They vote" (cited in Hauptman 1986a, 114).

In January a federal judge ruled that government supervisors could enter Allegany, and the Senecas' appeal of this decision was denied. In protest of the violation of treaty rights, President Seneca rejected an invitation to march in President Eisenhower's inaugural parade. This received considerable publicity, and outside groups began to rally to the Seneca cause. Oliver LaFarge, president of the Association of American Indian Affairs, joined the Nation in requesting New York governor Averell Harriman to ask the corps to reconsider. Harriman's decision to side with the Senecas was praised by the Indian Rights Association, the Indian Committees of both

the New York and Philadelphia Yearly Meetings, and the Friends
Committee on National Legislation. Once again the Quakers were
coming to the aid of the Senecas. More support was forthcoming
from other Iroquois Nations. Although the Seneca Nation had left
the Six Nations Confederacy by virtue of the 1848 revolution, in
February 1957 the Confederacy Council adopted a resolution con-
demning the flooding of the Cornplanter Grant in Pennsylvania.

Continuing the public relations assault and attempting to fit
into America's stereotyped image of Indians, Cornelius Seneca was
photographed, replete with Plains Indian war bonnet, viewing the
1794 Pickering Treaty at the National Archives. Meeting with Seneca at the direction of President Eisenhower, Interior Secretary Sea-
ton promised the Senecas a "square deal." Seneca also appeared as
"Chief Seneca" on the national television program "To Tell the
Truth" as he tried to draw public attention to the question of the
dam (Hauptman 1986a, 114).

The focal point at this stage was the $800 million House Public
Works Appropriations Bill, which included a $1 million line item
for the Kinzua Dam. Governor Harriman urged the New York congressional delegation to oppose the dam and work for the deletion of
the Kinzua appropriation. By a vote of 122 to 43, the House rejected
the deletion. The Supreme Court would shortly point to this vote as
proof of congressional intent to unilaterally break the Pickering
Treaty protecting Seneca land from additional U.S. claims. Kinzua
Dam became a *fait accompli* on 19 June 1957.

Arthur Morgan's reputation was such that the corps could not
easily ignore his criticisms, so in November 1957 it agreed to hire an
independent firm, Tippetts-Abbett-McCarthy-Stratton of New
York, to evaluate its plan as well as Morgan's. Unknown to the Nation or Morgan at the time, the independence of the firm was
strongly suspect. Its founder and three of the four partners were former members of the corps, and for more than two decades the corps
was the firm's most important client (A. Morgan 1971, 321). Its report noted that although Morgan's alternatives would store more
water and produce 115 million more kilowatt hours, they would
cost between 25 and 38 percent more, require 51 to 108 percent
more land, and dislocate 150 to 180 percent more people than the
corps's proposed dam. Although the report stated no preference for

any of the plans, the indelible impression was left that Morgan's plans were too expensive; furthermore, the people to be dislocated were white (Hauptman 1986a, 113), and Congdon's point about these people being voters was not lost on legislators.

For a government with minimal expenses prior to 1956, the cost of the dam fight had a major impact. Hastily made leases with Pennzoil, easements for an Iroquois Gas pipeline, and an extension for the New York State Thruway (Interstate 90) provided funds to aid in the fight against the dam (Hauptman 1986a, 114; A. Morgan 1971, 319).

In February 1958 SNI attorney Edward O'Neill returned to federal court to request an injunction, claiming that a special act of Congress was required to break the Pickering Treaty, an action recommended by Oscar Chapman nearly thirty years earlier. In March U.S. District Judge Joseph McGarraghy denied O'Neill's request, finding that Congress had signaled its intent to override the treaty by authorizing the project and appropriating funds for it. In November the Senecas' appeal of the McGarraghy decision was denied. In June 1959 the Supreme Court refused review of the decision. All legal avenues to halt construction were now closed.

While the Seneca leaders and attorneys were involved in legal and political ploys to halt the dam, there was a growing realization by the people of Allegany that this time a dam would be built on the Allegheny River and that their homes and way of life were in jeopardy. Until this time, many Senecas firmly believed that the moral sanctity of the treaty would protect them. While some of this might be interpreted as threat denial, it was also a logical response to the extent that rumors of dams to be built, which had circulated since the 1920s, had never been true.

Despite the efforts of President Seneca to draw attention to the Nation, there was increasing feeling at Allegany that the Nation needed stronger leadership. While the results of the 1958 election, in which the presidency shifted to Allegany, could be interpreted as rejection of old leadership viewed as ineffectual in stopping the dam, the actual situation was more complex. Through no fault of their own, Seneca leaders were ill-equipped to take on the federal government. At the same time, younger leaders who were better educated and more experienced in non-Indian ways were waiting in the wings to assume leadership. Their ascent to positions of power was hastened, not caused, by the dam fight.

Leadership passed from the People's Party to the relatively new Veterans' Party. With women still disenfranchised, the core of the new party consisted of veterans from World War II and the Korean War, nearly all high school graduates with experience in urban areas (many were ironworkers) and the military. Their candidate for Seneca president was George Heron, a war hero with three citations for valor in World War II (Hauptman 1986a, 114). Heron and his Cattaraugus running mate, Basil Williams, were victorious and, as president and treasurer, respectively, served for six years.

CONGRESSIONAL APPROVAL FOR KINZUA DAM

Although all legal roadblocks to the construction of Kinzua Dam were now gone, the Senecas hoped that public pressure might lead the Army Corps to reconsider. More groups rallied to support the Senecas. Following an investigation by anthropologist Burt W. Aginsky of City College of New York, the American Civil Liberties Union urged Eisenhower to disapprove the dam. He did not. On 25 May 1960, the House passed a $4.5 million appropriation bill for the construction of Kinzua Dam by a vote of 398 to 18. Groundbreaking for the dam occurred on 22 October and was followed by an address by former Pittsburgh mayor and current Pennsylvania governor David Lawrence, who stated "[Kinzua Dam] will some day stand as a living, useful reminder of the first lesson of good government—the needs of human welfare come first" (cited in Hauptman 1986a, 121).

It is difficult, if not impossible, to see any concern for human welfare in the story of Kinzua to this point. Congressional concern was exclusively with appropriations and engineering. There was no involvement of congressional committees on Indian affairs, no consideration of the impact of removal (or the cost) on the Senecas or Seneca culture, no recognition that the thirty-thousand-acre Allegany Reservation would, after the construction of Kinzua, consist of only ten thousand acres of steep hills and ten thousand acres of water, the other ten thousand acres having been taken up by the congressional villages of whites imposed on the Nation in 1880.

In November 1960 John F. Kennedy was elected U.S. president, and Basil Williams (as Seneca presidential candidate) and George Heron (candidate for treasurer) led the Veterans' Party to its second consecutive victory. The following month the American Civil Liberties Union asked Kennedy to take immediate action to stop the dam. Although sympathetic to the Indians, Kennedy declined, due to what he felt was a "real and immediate" need for flood protection (Klein and Hoogenboom 1980, 511). Having just won a narrow victory in which Pennsylvania governor David Lawrence played a critical role, the president-elect was unlikely to veto one of the governor's pet projects.

Support for the Senecas came from the National Congress of American Indians, the American Indian Chicago Conference, and the Councils of the Cherokee and Oneida Nations, which expressed unanimous sentiment against breaking the Pickering Treaty (Hauptman 1986a, 115). *New York Times* columnist Brooks Atkinson was instrumental in rallying non-Indian support. In February 1961 he wrote the first of what would total eleven columns over the next three years, describing and deploring what was happening to the Senecas. Continuing the skillful manipulation of symbols begun under Cornelius Seneca, the Seneca Nation, on George Washington's birthday, asked Kennedy to investigate once more Morgan's suggested alternatives. The *Times* chose the same date for the first of its eight editorials on the Senecas.

Kennedy, referring to the Supreme Court decision, said dam construction would continue. In essence, the president punted responsibility for an increasingly unpopular action to the court. As several leading Seneca politicians pointed out, the Supreme Court merely said the dam *could* be built, not that it *had to* be. This fine but important distinction was ignored by both Eisenhower and Kennedy. Kennedy did, however, indicate his concern for the Seneca Nation by instructing the Army Corps to explore the recreational potential the dam might provide to the Senecas, to seek out additional land for the Nation, and to provide for special damages and assistance to relocatees.

The Philadelphia Yearly Meeting of Friends also increased the pace of its campaign. In April 1961 the organization undertook an emergency program to find a satisfactory solution to the problems posed by the dam. Sixteen Quakers began a silent vigil at the dam site in August, which continued through Labor Day. The Quakers also initiated a letter-writing campaign to public officials and newspapers throughout the country. Popular Cree folksinger Buffy Sainte-Marie included pointed references to Kinzua in two of her songs, "Now That the Buffalo's Gone" and "My Country 'Tis of Thy People You're Dying." In western New York and Pennsylvania most air play was devoted to Johnny Cash's song (LaFarge 1964) about the Senecas, entitled "As Long As the Grass Shall Grow." In appreciation, Cash was later adopted by the Turtle Clan.

Iroquoian scholars found themselves in a particular dilemma. Many were strongly opposed to the dam, yet William Fenton was a New York state employee. In deference to his position, the Annual Conference on Iroquois Research, which he had founded, refused to go on record in opposition to Kinzua Dam, to the great disappointment of many younger scholars (Hertzberg 1986). Many of them, however, did speak out as individuals and did work with the Seneca Nation in the following years. While Fenton himself has been faulted by many Allegany Senecas for not attacking the dam more forcefully, his open letter (Fenton 1960) to Congressman James Haley (D-FL), chair of the House Subcommittee on Indian Affairs, is the most precise and poignant of all public statements against the dam, as well as most reflective of the Nation's position. Fenton also prepared a two-hundred-page manuscript on the history and meaning of the Pickering Treaty for use by the attorney for the Seneca Nation. While public pronouncements and publicity-seeking activities were important in rallying support, the value of private initiatives to important politicians, though equally futile in the end, cannot be underestimated.

IMPACT OF REMOVAL ON FAMILIES

As the adults, many of whom had fought hard to stop Kinzua, now regrouped to fight for the best possible settlement, the children were left out of the process. Social scientists at the time concentrated on the adults (Fenton 1985a), so there are no contemporary reports of children's reactions. Many of the parents interviewed were unaware of the children's feelings because, as one frankly stated, "We were simply too busy." This is not a callous response; there were constant meetings—with the Army Corps, the SNI Council, the various committees set up by the Kinzua Planning Committee, as well as Longhouse doings and church services. The Pickering Treaty having been broken, the Allegany Senecas had learned that whatever good was to come from Kinzua would have to be fought for, and that although they had a solid coterie of outside supporters putting pressure on Congress, the outlines of the final settlement would have to be determined by the Nation itself. For some, this was an exciting, though stressful, time. For others, the realization that the communities they had known along the river would no longer exist prompted great anger as well as sadness.

All of the conflicting responses of the parents were transmitted to the children. Those who were preadolescent at the time recalled that their parents were frequently absent at night attending meetings and returned upset, speaking Seneca in hushed tones that the children could not understand, thereby increasing their distress. Some children learned about the dam and removal for the first time at school. One vividly recalled not believing the teacher and racing home expecting a parent to deny the story, only to have the mother tearfully acknowledge its truth. Parents' descriptions of their children's reactions were often at great variance with the children's own recollections. The parents nearly always underestimated the stress, fear, and anger experienced by the children, emphasizing instead their enthusiasm about new furniture, indoor plumbing, and other advantages. It is probable that the parents, trying to cope with their own grief, could not tolerate the additional burden of recognizing how seriously their children were affected.

Some children attempted to channel their feelings into political action. A young boy whose mother was extremely involved in the Nation's fight wrote a highly publicized letter to President Kennedy asking why the 1794 treaty had been broken. A brief reply, not addressing the points he raised, came from the corps. Twenty years later, laughing at his naiveté, he said, "I really thought someone would listen, that it would make a difference." He dates his continuing disillusion with politics to that time. Although he was not a political radical in the Nation, in the past he participated in anti-Vietnam war protests in Washington, so he was no stranger to U.S. political duplicity.

At Remember the Removal Day in 1984, the Seneca Nation's marking of the twentieth anniversary of removal, a young woman spoke tearfully of carrying her doll to each corner of her house to say goodbye. Many of the more traumatic recollections centered on school. Another person later remembered the teacher telling children about the dam and then turning off the lights and playing "As Long As the Grass Shall Grow." At the time the bodies were removed from the old cemetery next to the Indian School at Red House, the windows were covered with black material. Although the intent was obviously to reduce the possibility of upsetting the children, the result for many was precisely the opposite. For most children there was no mechanism with which to deal with the trauma they were experiencing. The schools did not provide a forum for discussion, although they did serve to transmit information. One teacher had his students build a model of a dam, complete with goldfish, in order to demonstrate the functions of a dam. A student, perhaps inspired by the Seneca meaning of "Kinzua" (fish on spear), reacted by promptly spearing the fish with a newly sharpened pencil!

Families also did not provide an environment amenable to dealing with grief. Some parents worked out their sorrow by becoming deeply involved in removal planning. Children in these families had a greater awareness of what was actually occurring, but this was achieved primarily by the inadvertent overhearing of parental discussions, rather than through family discussions. Others continued life as usual, denying the threat and not becoming involved in work that would force them to surrender their denial. Children in these situations, too, had no opportunity to work out their feelings. A number of parents emphasized what they saw as the advantages of removal, primarily material in nature—new houses, indoor plumbing, new schools—and ignored potentially negative emotional aspects. Emily Benedek (1993, 303) has noted that Navajo children in the second grade at Rocky Ridge School on the Navajo reservation were excited about improved housing following relocation from the Hopi partition lands in the 1980s. Some Seneca children, too, were enthusiastic about the new houses, but recognition of material improvement does not negate feelings of deep loss. Surprisingly, no individuals who were children at the time reported any discussions about the dam or its implications with their peers, so this means of dealing with grief was also not available.

Regardless of whether the children were severely traumatized by the prospect of removal or guardedly excited about it, a constant undercurrent of their recollections was the realization that life would be very different and the fear that some things would be permanently lost. The loss of land had then, and continues to have, major ramifications. People now in their thirties and forties remember older family members collecting medicines and flowers, the latter often for sale in white towns and cities, and family berrying expeditions, usually all-day, fun-filled affairs. They regret the loss of botanical knowledge, remember their grandmothers' descriptions of medicines and their growth cycles, and wish they had paid more attention. Now, although much of the land where the flowers, berries, and medicines once grew is under water, a few elders still go out to collect and use the remaining plants. The berrying parties seem to be a thing of the past, although a few families may take an afternoon off and go to some of the public "pick your own" farms.

Aside from the loss of old play areas along the river, children were also stressed by the thought of changing schools in midyear. Those in their final year at the Indian School were less disrupted because they would soon have been moving to an integrated school in Salamanca anyway. Younger students were slightly concerned about the change, although some looked forward to it with great anticipation. Many Senecas who were students at the time reported that once they changed schools, they had behavior problems, acting out their stress and anger about removal in the classroom. Other students denied this. Salamanca elementary school teachers had little experience with Indian students; there were no Indian teachers or administrators in the entire system and no Indian-oriented programs at any level. A new fourth-grade teacher, who previously had experience with Indians, reported that the Seneca children in her room were quite passive and presented few, if any, difficulties. The cultural sensitivity of this teacher may have precluded the kinds of problems experienced in other classrooms.

Elders were also severely affected psychologically. Because of the political shift to the new party, they were not in positions of major political power. Furthermore, Longhouse people had always eschewed participation in the political system. Less educated than their children, they felt that they would receive fewer of the benefits to be derived from the dam. Elders persisted longer in their denial of the inevitability of the dam, with some seeking supernatural sanction for their beliefs. One man insisted that the "little people" who lived in the Allegheny Valley would rise up and destroy the dam, although this veiled reference to witchcraft upset many Longhouse people since it was clearly contradictory to the message relayed by the Creator to Handsome Lake.

Contrary to the evidence in other removals, there was no increase in alcohol abuse prior to removal. Although there were several individuals who had long been known as problem drinkers and who probably were alcoholics, there was no widespread serious problem. It is possible, however, that the scattered nature of the housing made the problem less visible. The evidence for the immediate post-removal period, while somewhat equivocal, seems to indicate increased alcohol abuse. With new housing patterns, individual acts of drunkenness were more apparent and more of a threat to the community, thereby demanding public attention.

Increased mortality, indicative of physiological stress, primarily affected the elders of Allegany. Because removal occurred over a four-year period, and stress was incurred over a period of years both preceding and following relocation, mortality figures for the period from 1960 to 1968 need to be considered. While most reports of increased mortality focus on the post-removal period, because the Seneca experience was prolonged, pre-removal deaths should also be attributed to increased stress. Young and old alike recall increased deaths in this period. Many tell of old people sitting on their porches or in their living rooms, staring out the windows and dying "of a broken heart." Even some of the elders who were initially interested in the move fit into this category.

Sociocultural stress occurred in several areas. Removal of forty-two graveyards, many of which were family plots designated as SNI cemeteries in August 1963, symbolized the total relocation. Among the first problems faced by the Nation was the establishment of two new cemeteries, whose locations were chosen by a committee composed of councilors and other citizens appointed by the Tribal Council in March 1962. Reinterment permits were signed by next-of-kin, where known and available, until November, at which time the Nation processed all of them. In September the council approved a contract with the federal government for the relocation of the estimated three thousand graves at a cost of $14.40 per reinterment.

The political changes necessitated by the dam were widespread. In addition to the party change discussed previously, the entire SNI government began an irreversible march toward an institutionalized bureaucracy. By 1962 the council, which previously had met twice a year, was meeting monthly. In order to coordinate activities, in June 1962 the Seneca Nation appointed its first ever full-time employee when former president and current treasurer George Heron was named administrator. The Kinzua Planning Committee, consisting of the SNI executive branch as well as at least six councilors plus other volunteer appointees, was in charge of planning the relocation, although its decisions required the council's approval.

Women played a significant role as committee members despite the fact that they were denied suffrage within the SNI at the time. These committees would prove to be the places in which women fine-tuned their skills and developed savvy in the Seneca political arena.

Two non-Senecas played important roles at this time as they too were involved full time in the relocation process. Sidney Carney, a Choctaw with a master's degree in accounting, was sent by the BIA to aid the Nation. Carney's arrival was initially met with some misgivings, but his willingness to bring his family and settle in Salamanca soon proved that he was not just another government bureaucrat on a brief visit. Years later, in 1986, his son, Dr. Mark Carney, returned to Allegany to head the Health Clinic in Steamburg, and the elder Carneys frequently return to spend summers in the area and visit their Seneca grandchildren.

In September 1962 Walt Taylor, the non-Quaker former head of the American Friends Service Committee, who had been spending several days each month at Allegany, moved with his family to Salamanca to begin work as the representative of the Indian Committee of the Philadelphia Yearly Meeting. Sidney Carney and Taylor remained with the Senecas until the mid-1960s, providing critical experience and advice until the Nation had a solid governmental framework in place with its own people in positions of authority.

Relocation of the Coldspring Longhouse presented a unique problem. Because the Army Corps had never been involved in the relocation of a church, the Nation undertook the move itself. The site was chosen in the Steamburg area, which was near its old location. Although two Longhouses had been abandoned in the early decades of the century, these were either not remembered or had been abandoned without elaborate rituals, so there was no model for the current relocation.

Because of problems created by what Senecas felt were inaccurate and unfair reports in the media at Allegany, whites were barred from the ceremony. A Seneca anthropologist was present and reported the event (Abrams 1967). Representatives of all Iroquois Longhouses in Canada and the United States met at Tonawanda to plan the ceremony, which took place on 2 June 1965. It was attended by several hundred, including Christians and formal representatives from each Longhouse. Corbett Sundown, a prominent chief at Tonawanda, led the ceremony, which began at 10:30 A.M. and lasted for nine hours. It ended with the Great Feather Dance at the old Longhouse and a cavalcade to the new one at Steamburg. According to Abrams (24), the "moving of the fire" showed the continuing religious cohesiveness of the followers of Handsome Lake, a reaffirmation of Iroquois religious identity. Additionally, the composition of the ceremony incorporated basic elements of other ceremonies sanctioned by Handsome Lake, such as wampum, the Thanksgiving Speech, and tobacco burning. Several current Longhouse leaders recalled with awe the emotion generated by the final Great Feather Dance at the old Longhouse; for them it has become the standard of comparison for all later Longhouse doings.

The end of the Red House Indian School was another source of stress. Its effect on the children has been discussed, but their parents were confronted with deciding what was to replace it. While many parents preferred to retain an all-Indian elementary school, the final committee decision, backed by the Tribal Council, was to build a new, integrated elementary school in the west end of Salamanca. It was named the Seneca Elementary School by Toni Biscup, a first grader at the Indian School.

Two major dilemmas faced the Seneca Nation in the early 1960s, one essentially political, the other cultural. First, the Nation needed to organize and fight for the highest possible settlement with Congress, but in deciding what to fight for, the Nation would commit itself to a path of development not easily changed in future decades. Second, although some women had begun to serve on committees and were employed by the Nation as secretaries, with largely administrative functions, they remained voteless. A referendum on women's suffrage was voted down in October 1962 for the third time in six years. Until 1964, the role of women in relocation remained advisory and instrumental.

The committees formulated by the council in 1962 indicated the Nation's priorities: Cemetery, Land Acquisition, Housing and Relocation, Recreational Development, Tangible and Intangible Damages, Lieu Lands. While these committees tended to be dominated by the same two dozen individuals throughout their existence, there was opportunity for significant input from others. The *Kinzua Planning Newsletter*, which began in 1961 and was edited by Jack Preston and later Walt Taylor, detailed the concerns and actions of the Kinzua Planning Committee and raised issues for popular discussion. The newsletter provided a major focus for community action, with eighteen hundred copies mailed out on at least a monthly basis. It was also sent to interested Quakers and other Seneca supporters and provided information for those writing letters to Congress and the media.

The newsletter also provided an outlet for children in that the cover of each mimeographed, multipage document was a drawing by a young Seneca, frequently the son or daughter of a deeply involved adult. Several of these young people, such as Carson Waterman, are now highly regarded craftspeople or artists, both within the Seneca Nation and the Iroquois community in general. Another mechanism used to increase community involvement was the sponsoring of contests, such as naming the new cemeteries or the new school, which provided small prizes and tended to focus community attention on the problems at hand. It should be noted that the idea of a newsletter was not new; one had been in existence at Allegany for years, but it was concerned primarily with social activities and community news. The new newsletter supplanted the old but differed in its singular focus. It also served to defuse potential problems by its institution of an anti-rumor column, addressing popular misconceptions before they produced major disruptions or divisions.

By late 1962 it was clear that the primary need to be addressed was housing for the people who would be removed. Choice of relocation sites was not difficult since little adequate land (relatively flat and above 1,365 feet, the maximum pool height behind the dam) remained for the Nation. A third of the reservation was taken up by the congressional villages, and the flood pool would take up another third, leaving behind mostly steep hills. Although individuals were free to settle among the hills, this was not a viable option since the Army Corps refused to pay the costs of providing access roads to homesites not in designated relocation areas. The corps also told the Senecas not to relocate in areas designated for a new four-lane, limited-access highway to replace the old two-lane Route 17. The New York State Department of Transportation and the corps appear to have collaborated closely in planning for the road, and the Nation's fight to stop the new highway was ultimately futile.

In June the Kinzua Planning Committee recommended two areas as relocation sites, one near Steamburg and Coldspring, the other, Jimersontown, near the old village of Shongo, adjacent to the west end of Salamanca. These sites were formally approved by the Tribal Council in August. Each contained three hundred acres of land above the 1,365-foot contour, although Steamburg (as it came to be known) is lower in elevation, and certain tracts there with poor drainage have had an almost constant flooding problem. At the same time, the council established the Seneca Nation Housing Authority to provide public housing for those not eligible for a relocation house, such as renters. The public housing was to be interspersed with the relocation housing and also included the construction of units at the Cattaraugus Reservation.

The public relations strategy continued. On American Indian Day in September 1962 the Temperance League sponsored a motorcade to visit the dam site, the old Quaker School at Tunessasa, and the monument to Cornplanter given by the Commonwealth of Pennsylvania in recognition of his aid. The Nation adopted Robert Haines of the Philadelphia Yearly Meeting and Congressman John Saylor (R-PA), the sole member of the Pennsylvania congressional delegation to oppose the dam, as honorary Senecas. Both adoptees wore Plains Indian–style war bonnets. In December George Heron appeared on the nationally syndicated *Today Show*. Congressman James Haley (D-FL), chair of the House Subcommittee on Indian Affairs, introduced House Resolution 1794 on 10 January 1963. It was not a coincidence that the number of the resolution was the date of the broken treaty. Twenty-seven months after the dam construction began, Congress finally turned its attention to the "human welfare" that Pennsylvania governor David Lawrence spoke of during the groundbreaking. Even today, Seneca elders and many young people point out that the Pennsylvania Railroad received the final payment of its twenty million dollars to relocate railroad tracks six months before Congress began to concern itself with the Senecas. In meetings with the New York congressional delegation and the BIA, the Nation learned that no monies would be available to it for the 1963 building season, although only two building seasons remained prior to the closing of the dam gates.

In the meantime, the Nation had been extremely busy planning for the future. The first meeting of the Economic Development and Employment Subcommittee in January 1963 made it clear that the Nation wanted its members employed in clearing the relocation sites and building the houses. The Education Committee, through school guidance counselors, distributed questionnaires to Indian students in grades seven through twelve on their plans and needs in order to determine its future educational program.

Walt Taylor resigned as newsletter editor in February in order to devote more time to personal contacts, particularly in the area of relocation housing. He was replaced by Merrill Bowen, head of the Cornplanter Landowners' Association. The Kinzua Planning Committee adopted a housing plan that called for subdivision of the relocation sites into primarily one-acre lots, with a maximum lot size of three acres. (See map 3 for a plan of the Steamburg relocation area.) Each site was shaped like an extended figure eight, with two loops joined by a center road along which public facilities were to be located. Churches were given preference in site choice, which was determined by lottery. Since the land proposed for the relocation sites was already allotted to individual Senecas, the Tribal Council, in April 1963, authorized that the allotted lands within the relocation areas would be recalled or condemned by the Nation if the landowners would not negotiate a sale. No federal funds were involved in the Nation's purchase of this land, and no houses were involved. Because the market value payment by the corps was insufficient for new homes of adequate quality and size, the housing plan called for payment based on compensation to individuals by the corps and SNI subsidy.

Besides building houses, the Nation also began to consider community facilities, such as tribal offices and community recreational buildings for both reservations. In May the council requested an additional $250,000 from the BIA to cover increased expenses for offices rented in Salamanca, attorneys' fees, publication of the *Kinzua Planning Newsletter*, and the hiring of a firm to appraise the old homes.

Much of the work done by SNI committees and subcommittees in the period 1960–63 was to determine the extent of compensable losses that would be sustained by individuals and the Nation. This required not only determination of loss but also assignment of dollar value and the proposal of programs to alleviate the losses and for rehabilitation, which would be inserted into H.R. 1794 as tangible and intangible damages. It also had the effect of bringing the Nation into contact with dozens of state and federal agencies, appraisal firms, utilities, and consultants of all kinds. A cursory survey indicated forty-three of these contacts, some brief, some prolonged. Although the Nation would probably have been in a stronger position had it been able to field more experienced negotiators and planners, Taylor's and Carney's advice helped it avoid some obvious pitfalls. More importantly, this provided a valuable learn-as-you-go experience, limited only by the fact that so much learning was cramped into a very small time frame and mistakes could not easily be undone.

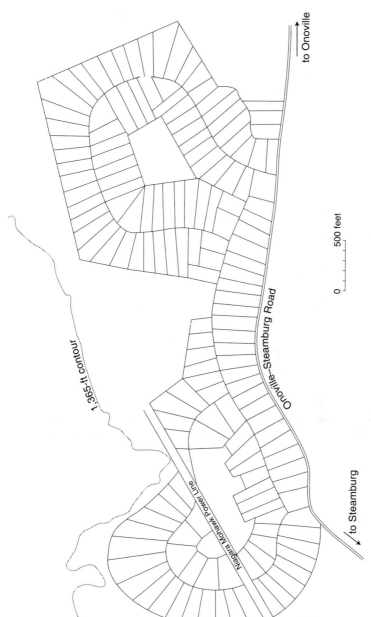

to Onoville

1,365-ft contour

Onoville–Steamburg Road

Niagara Mohawk Power Line

to Steamburg

0 500 feet

3. Plan of Steamburg Relocation Area

Once relocation sites had been chosen and divided into lots, the focus of housing shifted to individual families. The first decision to be made was that of relocation site. Although the Christian churches had chosen to relocate to Jimersontown and the Longhouse to Steamburg, religious preference was only a consideration, not a major determinant of site choice. Families with adult members employed in Salamanca or Buffalo tended to choose Jimersontown since it was closer to their work. Jimersontown was also the choice of families with children in high school, since relocation there would allow their participation in after-school activities; some families with younger children made the same choice in order to avoid long bus rides to and from school. Proximity to the "old places," as they are now called, also influenced some families, particularly those who still retained some land above 1,365 feet and wanted to continue to use it.

Choice of lot within each site was determined by lottery, with those drawing low numbers choosing first. Lots were drawn on 29 September at the Coldspring Longhouse and 30 September at the Shongo courthouse. At that time, forty-one people drew lots for Steamburg and thirty-seven for Jimersontown, although more lots were chosen later. Only those who had houses were eligible for relocation housing, so this spurred attempts by a number of families to quickly build houses on old foundations in order to be eligible. The size of the relocation house depended upon the number of bedrooms needed. The value of the old home was prorated in terms of the appraisal value set by the corps against a schedule of subsidies to a maximum of fifteen thousand dollars. As Fenton (1967, 17) pointed out, those with the least stood to gain the most. In order to limit speculation, any family receiving a subsidy from the Nation that sold its relocation house within ten years was required to repay a proportion of that subsidy. Where children had built homes on parental land, that land was often transferred to the children so that they would be eligible for land as well as housing. People with multiple houses were entitled to multiple replacement homes, but since some of these houses were rented, a number of homeowners offered to sell both land and house to the renters in order to make them eligible for benefits. There is no indication of major attempts at profiteering. Most land transactions represented formal recognition of changes that had occurred many years before, when transfers were sealed by a handshake and registration with the Nation was an often ignored formality. Those who quickly built shack-type housing were usually those who were living in crowded conditions with friends or relatives and who probably would have built similar housing eventually. Property transactions, in general, reflected creative approaches to longstanding problems and were marked by a good deal of concern for the welfare of individuals, families, and communities.

By November 1963 much of the planning was completed. Bids for road construction to the sites had been awarded, and the first family, the Clinton Redeyes, had moved due to relocation of the Erie Railroad. The Land Acquisition, Lieu Lands, Tangible and Intangible Damages, Public Facilities, and Cemetery Committees, along with the Economic Development Subcommittee, had all completed their assignments. Of the early committees, only Housing and Relocation, Educational Scholarship, and Recreational Development were still active, along with a new committee on Industrial Development. Recognizing the increased stress experienced by Allegany residents, who now knew where they were going to live but not the house type, since that had yet to be decided, the Cattaraugus County Welfare Department added a new social worker for the Allegany Reservation in early December.

Undercurrents of racism against the Senecas, particularly in the city of Salamanca, became more apparent in 1963 when the outlines of the final settlement, especially the rehabilitation funds, became widely known. Some children, primarily those in the integrated schools, were the focus of disparaging talk about "rich Indians." In some cases this led to physical fights; as one young man who later left the area stated, "You can only be called a 'squaw man' so many times before you fight back." Schoolyard taunts, while infrequent, reflected adult attitudes that were probably prompted by jealousy. One prominent white businessman told Congressman Haley's subcommittee during hearings held over the summer in both Salamanca and Washington: "I am opposed to giving them any additional land because they have had thirty thousand acres to rattle around on for all these years, and if you are going to improve their lot, you are not going to improve it by giving them some more land to roam around on and do nothing" (House 1964, 43). A balance to this perspective was provided by Walt Taylor in his testimony: "The Allegany Reservation of the Seneca Nation of Indians, however, is no mere section of real estate. It is a way of life. When you cut off part of a living body it makes a difference whether you amputate a limb or a head. The Kinzua Dam comes dangerously close to chopping off the head of the Seneca way of life" (254). While it is clear from the testimony during the hearings that many whites in the area were far from sympathetic to their Seneca neighbors, it is equally clear that they felt they too would derive benefits from the settlement, primarily in terms of economic advantages. The same white businessman who objected to a land settlement for the Senecas said, "This is just going to be the greatest thing that ever happened out here" (45).

The selection of individual relocation sites was completed by February 1964, with approximately half the relocatee families choosing Steamburg and half Jimersontown. The Tribal Council had decided that the Nation would take a $10 per acre option for land settlement but waived any interest in compensation for improvements (e.g., houses, barns, privies). When the corps filed the Declaration of Taking for each parcel, it deposited with the Registry of the Federal District Court of Western New York an amount it considered fair market value. Tribal members who had reached agreement with the corps and were not seeking SNI subsidy for relocation housing could withdraw a maximum of 90 percent of the funds on deposit. Where homeowners and the corps were unable to negotiate a settlement, a binding determination was made by Empire Appraisal Associates. The remaining 10 percent was to stay on deposit until H.R. 1794 became law. For renters, the Tribal Council approved the construction of twenty-five public housing units at Allegany, all to be individual houses on half-acre lots with a hundred-foot frontage where possible.

By mid 1964 the House and Senate were unable to reach agreement on H.R. 1794. In fact, the Conference Committee did not meet at all between 25 June and 12 August, and the Nation was reluctant to let building contracts without assurance of the necessary funds. The first contracts for houses (two in Jimersontown and three in Steamburg) were approved in July when the first payments for sixty-four tracts were received. At the same time, the corps agreed to postpone closing the dam gates until October. Much of the clearing of brush on house lots was done by Seneca boys under a youth work program. The costs of this program were to come from the indirect damage funds.

The final settlement, Public Law 88–533 (78 *Stat.* 738), was passed on 31 August 1964 and signed by President Lyndon Johnson the following day. The legislation was patterned after the Missouri River Basin bills for the Standing Rock, Crow Creek, Cheyenne River, and Lower Brule Reservations but was more favorable to the Indians. In explaining why the Seneca settlement was larger than previous Indian settlements and those with whites displaced by Kinzua, anthropologist Phileo Nash, the commissioner of Indian Affairs, stated "broken promises come high" (Senate 1964, 166). In broad outline, it contained the following provisions: to the Seneca Nation $666,285 for direct damages, $100,000 for damages caused by the increased expense of developing or exploiting oil and gas resources, $250,000 for reimbursable fees and expenses incurred in relation to the project, and $945,573 for all other claims; to individual Senecas a total of $522,775 as compensation for improvements on their land. Section 4 authorized the deposit of $12,128,917 at 4 percent annual interest in the U.S. Treasury to the credit of the Seneca Nation "to improve the economic, social, and educational conditions of enrolled members of the Seneca Nation." Commonly known as rehabilitation funds or section 4 monies, these were to be used for relocation, construction of sanitation facilities, houses, roads, community buildings and facilities, and industrial and recreational development on both SNI reservations. Mineral rights in the take area were reserved to the Nation, and individual Senecas could remain on the land until 1 January 1965, unless the secretary of the army granted an extension. Until sixty days prior to vacating the land, Senecas had the right to harvest crops, salvage timber and improvements, and remove sand and gravel. Because the final date for removal was three months away, this seemingly generous offer in reality gave them thirty-one days for all salvage work. The Nation was given the right to use and occupy the take area of the reservoir within the reservation for all purposes "not inconsistent with the interests in land acquired by the United States" (P.L. 88–533, Sec.

9). This included the right to license hunting and fishing by non-Senecas and regulate access to the shoreline, provided that free public access be provided. Because the land was taken as an easement, rather than by outright purchase, if the secretary of the army ever determined that all or part of the interests acquired were no longer necessary, all rights, interests, and the title would vest in the Seneca Nation (section 15).

Section 18 stated: "The Secretary of the Interior shall, after consultation with the Seneca Nation, submit to Congress a plan for complete withdrawal of Federal supervision over the property and affairs of the Nation and its members. Said plan shall be submitted within three years from the effective date of this Act." For nearly a decade the threat of termination was a cloud over the Seneca Nation, and its officials spent considerable time and effort successfully lobbying against implementation of this section, which would mean the end of treaty obligations and protections and the end of their tax-free status. Although the Nation was assured that termination would not occur without a referendum vote supporting it, a number of Senecas are still very uneasy about this provision, which, while not implemented, has not been repealed.

In September the Nation initiated the Seneca Nation Housing Enterprise for the Nation's building project, and the council gave it authority to act on behalf of the sni. Lloyd Barnwell, the Seneca superintendent of the project, began consultation with families on home selection. While for many middle-aged Senecas it was exciting to choose their house style (all variants of a single-level suburban ranch-style house) and such "extras" as paved driveways and garages, it was extremely stressful for elders. One Seneca woman was emotionally unable to continue recounting how she spent weekends helping elders try to understand the intricacies of indoor plumbing, electric wiring, and contemporary appliances. Most of her time was spent helping them cope with their grief and frustration rather than the mechanics of the new houses. Various outside agencies such as the Cattaraugus County Cooperative Extension provided people to discuss such topics as interior decorating and landscaping, although few took advantage of the opportunity. Other workshops on basic housekeeping and sewing were ignored as being useless by people already highly skilled in these areas and as implicitly racist and insulting by more socially and politically conscious individuals.

The final leave taking of the "old places" was often acutely traumatic for Senecas of all ages. Although the corps was supposed to give appropriate notice prior to razing and burning the houses, it was often short notice. The corps arrived at one home when the parents were in Olean, an hour's drive away, and told the children they would return at 5 P.M. to move the family. Unable to contact their parents, the children were deeply upset until the parents returned. One family, having had only a day's notice, was so busy that they forgot to inform their eldest child, who was away at college, that they had moved. Another family's pet dog was run over by a bulldozer, and although the corps replaced it with another dog, the children still vividly recall its loss. In at least a handful of cases, houses were razed and burned before the contents had been removed; some families lost only a few items of sentimental value, while at least one lost nearly everything. Some people walked away from their vacant homes and never looked back; Fenton (1967, 16) reported that one man tossed a match to his house as he left for the last time. Others made a point of returning as if to receive final confirmation of removal. One woman told of her grief while watching her adult son, married and with a family, break down and sob as he watched his home being destroyed. Today, recalling these events often precipitates highly emotional responses. A male elder tearfully pointed out his old place, visible now only as broken tree trunks above the water line, as he recounted his childhood. A woman who was a child at the time of relocation said she had begun to once again have dreams of her old home and life, which she directly related to her role in aiding this research.

Women, whose traditional work was in the domestic sphere and whose daily activities were reminders of what was about to be lost, discussed this period in more emotional terms than did men, who tended to emphasize the political aspects. However, it was during this period that women set the groundwork for their entrance into the formal political sphere.

FOUR

The "New Places": Broken Hearts

As William Fenton (1967) pointed out, the move to ranch-style houses in the relocation sites was actually the second housing revolution of the Senecas. In the eighteenth century they lived along the river in small settlements of matrilineal longhouses. The first revolution occurred a century later with the arrival of the Quakers, who believed the only way the Senecas could prevent further white encroachment on their land was to accept some white cultural patterns, in particular nuclear family residences and farming. The shift to log and shingle houses scattered along the river occurred relatively swiftly, but as Diane Rothenberg (1980, 74) points out, although several families may have taken to farming and dairying, the Senecas never became a nation of farmers. The second revolution, necessitated by Kinzua Dam, was essentially a return to the pre- and protohistoric pattern of nucleated villages (Fenton 1967, 10).

The most obvious change resulting from removal was the material improvement in housing. The "old places," described by one man as "wrinkled but nice," varied from small, one-room tar paper shacks to substantial two-story houses with porches and outbuildings. Although only five families in the take area had received public assistance in the first eleven months of fiscal year 1962, the county welfare agent estimated that over half the families shared in the monthly distribution of surplus foods (Fuhriman 1963, 18). The differences in median income of families consisting of two adults and two children between Senecas in the take area, $3,900, and their Anglo neighbors in Cattaraugus County, $5,606 (17), while obviously significant, should not be used to overstate the relative poverty of the Senecas. In addition to cash income, the Indians made considerable use of free natural resources. Fuhriman's survey (20) indicates that all the families utilized wild herbs, 65 percent hunted deer, 62 percent used wild fruits, and 34 percent fished. Firewood was a particularly important resource, as over three-quarters of the houses were heated by wood and a third used it for cooking (28). Most of the houses had electricity (96 percent), refrigerators (93 percent), televisions (81 percent), washing machines (79 percent), and telephones (51 percent). The number of washers is surprising since less than half of the houses had a well or water on the premises, and only 21 percent had a flush toilet and bath (24). All of the relocation houses had electricity and an indoor water supply, which were greatly appreciated by young and old alike, who did not miss hauling water or late-night trips to the outhouse in the dead of winter. Today, Senecas who remember the "old places" point to improved housing as the primary benefit derived from relocation.

Although by 1968 the Allegany Senecas probably did have, as George Heron suggested, the best Indian housing in the country, it was not without its drawbacks. Modern housing was stressful to many, but especially for the elders trying to cope with monthly utility and insurance bills as well as increased food and housing costs. A number of families, not used to monthly budgets, splurged on "extras" and then found themselves hard-pressed to repay government (SNI) subsidies. Additional problems resulted from the inundation of the areas that had produced most of the wild fruits and berries. Because collecting expeditions had been important social occasions, this loss had ramifications well beyond the purely economic. Hunting, particularly in Jimersontown, was more difficult. As one man told Fenton (1967, 15), "Who wants to drag a deer taken out of season into a housing development?" Several people recalled with humor the plight of one young hunter who was arrested for dragging the bear he had legally shot through the streets of Salamanca back to his home in Jimersontown.

There were also differences between the two relocation sites that have become more apparent with time. Jimersontown, abutting the city of Salamanca, was distinctly more suburban, even to the extent of purchasing water from the city. Schools, shops, gas stations, jobs, and recreational facilities were within a maximum thirty-minute walk. In addition, it became the focal point for the SNI government because the Council building containing the recreation hall was built there. This became more important as the bureaucracy increased, and the government became the major employer of Senecas.

Steamburg, on the other hand, was decidedly more rural than Jimersontown, with no public buildings except for the Longhouse and few plans for any. Deer were more plentiful in the hills, and hunting was easier. The nearest white settlement was the small village of Steamburg, less than a mile away, which provided none of the amenities of Salamanca. The twelve-mile distance between the two relocation centers suggested early that they might develop along different lines (Fenton 1967, 15). While it is easy to overestimate the degree of change, it should be noted that there were, prior to removal, concentrations of houses in the villages of Red House, Quaker Bridge, and Coldspring. Several people reported that there was some good-natured competition between the communities, particularly among teenaged boys. One even said there were minor linguistic differences (presumably in adolescent argot) that were indicative of residence. It can be argued, therefore, that the move to the two relocation communities was a change of degree rather than kind.

Although the actual relocation of families extended over a three-year period, the majority of families moved into their new houses in 1966. This had both advantages and disadvantages. People understood each other's problems since many were shared, but each family was intensely involved in its own particular adjustment. The new houses, constructed under the supervision of Lloyd Barnwell, an experienced builder, were actually built by large numbers of young Senecas learning the trade on the job, and as a result a number of houses required some remedial attention. There were charges at the time that inferior building materials were sometimes substituted for top-shelf materials as ordered by the Seneca Nation Housing Enterprise, although it is currently not possible to document this.

Besides the expected problems with the new houses, additional stress appeared in the sociocultural realm. Except on rare occasions, old neighbors tended to be separated, and the distance between relocation sites made travel difficult for those without cars. Once the four-lane, limited-access Route 17 was built, dissecting the reservation, and the years took their toll on the remaining old routes (which were often under water and not repaired when above it), this became a greater problem since hitchhiking and bicycles were technically illegal on the new road. Used to greater space between houses, nearly all relocatees reported a difficult time adjusting to close neighbors; a major complaint was the loss of privacy. As one man in the military stated, "When I left, my mother had forty acres along the river. When I returned, she had three acres . . . *three acres!*" Looking out the window and seeing a nearby house was a major change; more annoying to many was seeing someone else's dog in their yard. This complaint became more pronounced as some families began to plant flower and vegetable gardens.

Close neighbors also signaled the end of one of the most pleasurable recreations of the Allegany Senecas—visiting. Prior to relocation, visits were all-day affairs at which people exchanged social news and spent the time enjoying each other's company. As previously mentioned, the day-long berrying expeditions also became a thing of the past. People no longer needed a day to exchange information; what used to be told could now be observed. Proximity of houses, plus later the existence of public buildings in Jimersontown, also led to increased acts of vandalism, many of which were apparently perpetrated by adolescents. This was upsetting not only because of the repair costs involved but because it seemed to many to indicate a heretofore rare behavior problem at a time when the Senecas wished to prove to their often skeptical white neighbors that their new housing developments would not become rural ghettoes.

NEW COMMUNITY ORGANIZATIONS

Although prior to removal most organizations in which the Indians participated were predominantly Seneca (Fuhriman 1963, 33), the number and variety of these increased significantly. This strongly reflects the cultural involution predicted by the Scudder and Colson model (1982). The Seneca Nation government continued, and even increased, its involvement in a broader political spectrum, but the communities, on a cultural level, withdrew into themselves, forging new, often temporary, mechanisms that allowed them to confront the changes in their lives not as individuals but as Senecas. To a great extent these organizations seem to have replaced, insofar as possible, the visiting of previous years. Not surprisingly, they were more formal, with set dates and times of meeting and often with minimal dues and officers, reflecting the newly learned organizational skills of their founders. The development and decline of many of these organizations indicate their progression into the third stage of the Scudder and Colson model. As the Senecas began to feel more "at home" in their new communities, as they developed new individual means of coping with the stress of relocation, or as it diminished, the organizations became less necessary, and most of them disappeared. Those that addressed concerns of a more enduring, less removal-oriented, nature (e.g., problems of elders, recreation, political action) continued, frequently replaced by formal government departments. To the same extent that organizational demise signaled the end of the second stage, the range of organizations indicated the cultural priorities and concerns of the relocatees.

Most of the organizations met on at least a monthly basis. Among the most active was the "21 Plus" group, which held biweekly potluck dinners, often followed by bingo or other recreational activities. The core membership was drawn from those young and middle-aged adults who were active in fighting the dam or planning relocation, and meetings provided a relaxed setting in which mutual problems could be discussed and old friends and neighbors could establish new patterns of socialization. While apolitical, membership tended to represent those couples who had decided to capitalize as best as possible on the benefits of relocation. They were not, however, people who welcomed removal. Confronted with the inevitability of relocation, their response was to try to direct the change in the least disruptive direction. Perhaps because of their previous involvement in removal and the continuation of social ties in the new communities, this group was able to deal with their grief more effectively and adapt to the new situation more quickly. That this club in particular was related to the stress of removal is demonstrated by its disappearance by the end of 1972.

Currently many of the surviving members (and their children) occupy mid- to high-level administrative positions in the Nation or are employed in relatively high-paying positions outside.

The concerns of many of the elders were met by the "Seniors" group, which has remained very active. In addition to monthly meetings, the Seniors often organized bus trips to concerts in Buffalo and elsewhere and multiday excursions to Washington DC or Toronto. There is no evidence that the group's participants represented a particular political philosophy. It is likely that they were similar to the 21 Plus members except in age. The increased mortality noted for elders may have removed many of the more traditionalist potential members.

The Allegany Singing Society, the social society associated with the Coldspring Longhouse, was also very active through 1972. While this early post-removal activity may well reflect the stress of removal, it should be noted that the Singing Society's visibility in the community is also a reflection of the charisma and organizational skills of its chosen leader. Although the society provided a social and recreational outlet for members of the Longhouse, its contributions to the relocation communities, especially Steamburg, were important, and its popularity probably reflects removal-related stress. Among other things, the society provided financial and material aid to needy families, cleared and grubbed lots, and organized a house preparation and welcome home for a seriously wounded Viet Nam veteran.

Concern for adolescents and children is shown in the formation of a series of clubs for this age group, most of which were of short duration. The Teens Club lasted until 1971, with an unsuccessful attempt at revival in the mid 1970s. Finding chaperones and transportation for activities presented chronic problems. Some of the intended functions of this club were taken over by a Girl Scout troop, which lasted until 1972. A Boy Scout troop and Cub Scout pack also flourished from 1969 to 1972. In general, recreational activities for young people were seriously hampered by the distance between the relocation sites, as it was always necessary to provide transportation for the Steamburg children since most activities tended to be centered in Jimersontown. Attempts to circumvent this problem by forming clubs at each site tended to be unsuccessful since the pool of potential members was too small. Adults at Jimersontown and Steamburg with their own vehicles were able to interact as frequently as they wished, thereby keeping strong ties between the two communities. That children were less able to do this may have been partially responsible for some of the current differences between the sites.

Interest in sports has always been high at Allegany, and in the immediate post-removal period (pre-1970) there were many attempts to organize softball, baseball, basketball, and lacrosse teams for teens and adults of both sexes. Although most of these met with ultimate failure, there was always a team of some kind for young people, especially boys, to join. The creation of the Seneca Nation Recreation Department in 1976 provided a format for continuing participation in athletics that has been extremely successful. By sponsoring teams in a variety of sports as well as supervising athletic facilities, the department has provided a stability for recreational activities previously missing. In addition, the program provides a safe, supervised environment for children. Awards to outstanding Seneca athletes are an important mechanism for enhancing self-esteem. Snowsnake and lacrosse have never been formally reestablished, although they were popular prior to removal (Fuhriman 1963, 34), and the Golden Eagles lacrosse team of the nearby Cattaraugus Reservation has won several championships in the Iroquois Nationals. To some extent, at least for older children, high school sports activities provided an important recreational outlet, with eighteen Seneca students (not all of whom were relocatees) on teams in 1969. The greatest concentration of Seneca students (seven) was on the boys track team; most activities had only one Indian participant. Reflecting cultural norms of the late 1960s, athletics was primarily a male activity. There were also seven Seneca members on the student council. Again, however, residence in Steamburg may have limited participation in extracurricular activities.

By 1967 the *Kinzua Planning Newsletter* was replaced by *Oh-He-Yoh-Noh* (People of the Beautiful River, or Allegheny People) as a community newsletter that covered social activities, political developments in the Nation and on state and federal levels, and commentary by individuals. Although there had been a newsletter (*Council Fires*) prior to the *Kinzua Planning Newsletter*, *Oh-He-Yoh-Noh* was much longer and covered a greater variety of topics. Supported solely by contributions, it represented a major means of increasing community awareness and involvement. Most of the activities announced occurred in Jimersontown, although participation by Steamburg residents was encouraged, and it was apparent by 1967 that Jimersontown would become the social as well as political hub of the Allegany Reservation. The first news about Steamburg, in a brief column, did not appear until April 1968. There are at least two explanations for this. Distribution was much easier in Jimersontown since each house had a mailbox (for rural delivery, Salamanca) in which the paper could be placed. Steamburg residents did not have mail delivery and had to go a minimum of one-half mile to the small post office in the town of Steamburg, thus necessitating a house-by-house delivery of the newsletter. There is still no mail delivery in Steamburg, another indication of the differences between the two sites. A second reason provided by several Senecas was that Steamburg was dominated by Longhouse adherents, who participated less in these activities. While religion did not seem to be an important factor in determining choice of relocation area, approximately three-quarters of the first Steamburg residents were Longhouse people. Government activities were also centered at Jimersontown, and most Longhouse people did not participate in government affairs. One man who was on the Tribal Council in the mid 1960s said the focus on Jimersontown reflected a widespread belief that the Longhouse people wanted to be left alone and that the council respected their wishes. It is not clear how accurate this assessment was; however, it is still a prevalent attitude.

RELATIONS WITH NON-INDIANS

Another important factor at this time was the arrival of the first of two VISTA couples in 1966. Nancy and Lew Spaulding are still remembered by many; in some ways they filled the void left by the departure in 1965 of Walt and Peggy Taylor of the Indian Committee of the Philadelphia Yearly Meeting. Resident in the community, the Spauldings pitched in and helped in many community activities;

they suggested and organized others. In December 1967 they arranged the first community-wide children's Christmas party, a tradition that continues under the direction of the Seneca Nation Recreation Department. They also began plans for a Head Start nursery, which also continues, now under the direction of the Seneca Nation Education Department. They were particularly helpful in providing transportation between the two communities. Unlike the myriad "experts" and consultants who flocked to Allegany in the late 1960s, the Spauldings are recalled primarily as friends, and their contributions to the reservation have been far more substantial than those of the specialists.

The personal quality of these relationships increased in importance as the Senecas found themselves besieged by outsiders. One young man stated that school children used to compare visiting social scientists and that he thought for a while that the Senecas were becoming Navajos, with each family consisting of parents, children, and a social scientist. In this time of cultural involution, unknown outsiders were viewed with distrust and suspicion as the Indians and their new houses became objects of curiosity. An ad in June 1968 in the Allegany State Park paper suggested visitors go see the Indians in their relocation homes, and the editor of *Oh-He-Yoh-Noh* warned the people to "get prepared to be on exhibit again." At approximately the same time the Corps of Engineers suggested a Seneca Indian Day at Kinzua Dam, an incredibly callous, though presumably well-intentioned, assault on a people still trying to cope with removal. The editor stated that the only appropriate response would be to tell the corps to "go jump in the lake." The day was never held. Since the editors of *Oh-He-Yoh-Noh* tended to be women who were trying to make the best of removal, the strength of these reactions indicated that similar feelings were pervasive at Allegany. To a lesser extent the curiosity continued; the summer 1986 *Chautauqua-Allegany Travel Guide* suggested a drive through the relocation sites (map included) for tourists. Carloads of non-Indians driving slowly through the Steamburg relocation site during this period still sparked anger and resentment in residents. Several times I was asked if a particular car belonged to friends seeking my campsite as Senecas tried to identify the strangers in their community. This suggestion was not present in the 1987 version, possibly because the format was different.

In 1969 the Tribal Council took formal action, barring the news media from its meetings, due in part to negative stories and misquotes by a reporter from the *Olean Times*. Senecas were urged to attend council meetings but not to give information to outsiders because of their lack of discretion. Similar problems confronted the Longhouse, where whites were not welcome for a brief period. It is important to note that prior to 1966 Seneca anger and resentment were directed at the federal government and explicitly did not have ethnic overtones. Later, as the new communities were established, anti-white sentiment was related to provocation by whites as well as attempts to establish Seneca identity in changed surroundings.

POLITICAL INVOLVEMENT

Prior to 1970, the involvement of Seneca individuals and leaders in the political and social activities of the surrounding areas, especially Salamanca, was minimal. Perhaps reflecting the desire of white communities to share in the benefits of the dam, particularly the Senecas' section 4 monies, George Heron was elected to the Board of Directors of the Salamanca Area Industrial Development Corporation. Two years later, he and Tom Hunt, president of the corporation, were named Citizens of the Year by the Salamanca Jaycees. In 1965 SNI president Basil Williams was named the Seneca Nation's representative to the Cattaraugus County Community Action Program. By 1969 it was clear that individual Senecas were becoming involved in areas not directly related to economic development. In 1969, demonstrating his interest in education, Robert Hoag became the first Indian to run for a seat on the school board and lost by only forty votes. Cornelius Abrams Jr., appointed to the Cattaraugus County Planning Board, also ran for justice of the peace on the Democratic ticket, although a number of Senecas at the time questioned the wisdom of political activity at both Nation and county levels. This did, however, direct the local Democratic Party to recognize the potential influence of Seneca voters, and it did take out several small political ads in *Oh-He-Yoh-Noh*.

The changed physical environment was another source of stress. Many of the flowers that women would collect and sell in Bradford or Buffalo were gone, as were many of the medicines. People complained of being sick more frequently. Timber, for firewood or basket splints, was less plentiful and more distant. Despite evidence to the contrary from New York State, there was a deep-seated belief that the soil at the new sites was not fertile, so few people planted gardens, thus incurring additional food expenses. By the 1980s this had changed considerably, due in part to a vigorous community garden plan developed by the Seneca government, the success of which surprised even its sponsors. In addition to community plots, there were lush gardens of corn, beans, squash, tomatoes, cucumbers, and onions behind many homes. The weather and crop yields were a frequent topic of conversation, and sharing of surplus produce with nongardening friends and neighbors was common. While people had enjoyed going to the banks of the river, going to the reservoir was often unpleasant due to the fact that the abandoned lands were being used as a dumping ground by both whites and Indians. Drag racing along the abandoned roads was also common until the Tribal Council moved to put a stop to it. For many this was just one more unpleasant reminder of how life along the "beautiful river" had changed.

Other changes occurred in the formal political structure, with women finally, in 1964, gaining the right to vote. In 1966 they were given the right to hold office. It is not clear what effect, if any, the Kinzua fight had on this. It is probable that the main impetus was the social agenda of the 1960s and that Kinzua only hastened the inevitable. One obvious effect of the dam was that women, once enfranchised, took a much shorter time to move into the political arena. Because of the mobilization necessitated by the fight, there were women who were politically skilled and knowledgeable, resulting in only a five-year gap between women being permitted formal political participation and the appearance of the Nation's first female councilor, Alice Jean Jemison of Cattaraugus, appointed by President William Seneca to fill an unexpired term. The executive post of clerk has been held by women since 1974, and women are most frequently elected to the positions of surrogate and peacemaker. Phoebe Crouse, elected treasurer in 1972, was the first woman to head a reservation.

APPLYING THE SCUDDER-COLSON MODEL

The Allegany Seneca experience indicates that Scudder is correct in his return to a four-stage model. Although plans for a dam were discussed periodically for half a century, serious consideration only began in the early 1950s. Unlike many Third World societies, the Senecas were aware of the threat and mobilized to counter it. This is probably more common in literate, politically centralized societies.

Another variation in the proposed model is suggested by the Seneca data. While it is clear that the people themselves were still in the Adjustment and Coping stage before 1970, the government was well into the stage of Community Formation and Economic Development. This distinction between cultural and more narrowly defined political stages is critical. For the Senecas the distinction is a direct outgrowth of the form of the stage and the federal political process. Because of the prolonged fight against the dam and Seneca participation in the formulation of House Resolution 1794, particularly the amount and disposition of rehabilitation funds, the political leaders were required to move into areas of initiative and risk taking even before removal had occurred. The failure to do so would have resulted in either severely reduced section 4 monies or possible per capita distribution of the federal settlement. The latter option had disastrous results in other Indian nations, and the Senecas rejected this, although some nonresident enrollees favored it. Because, like other Senecas, the political leaders were suffering the stress of dislocation as they began to plot the future of the postdam Seneca Nation, they were more reliant on outside advice and direction than they might have been without it. Cushioning the stress at the political level was the fact that half the leaders were from Cattaraugus and were not relocatees. Aside from the rehabilitation funds, the social programs of the New Frontier and Great Society also became available to the Seneca Nation at this time, thereby making it difficult to sharply distinguish between the effects of the dam (rehabilitation funds) and changes that would have been possible anyway (e.g., Head Start, Community Action Programs). The organization required by the dam fight put the Nation in a much better position to effectively utilize these newly available programs. Whether the Seneca Nation would have taken advantage of them in the absence of Kinzua can only be conjecture.

As the people were learning to cope with new houses, schools, and neighbors, their elected leadership was moving to closer interaction with the federal government. Allegany society was still in a stage of cultural involution, wary of outside influences and strengthening old ties of friendship and kinship; Allegany government had moved into the following stage of Economic Development. While to a great extent the focus of the sni government during the period from 1959 to 1966 was the Allegany relocation, it is important to remember that the government also represented the more populous Cattaraugus Reservation. Rehabilitation funds were given to the Nation as a whole, and residents of Cattaraugus were also interested in participating in newly evolving federal programs. Seneca leaders could not afford to become bogged down in the local aftermath of removal.

FIVE

Making It in the Great Society

As the previous chapter demonstrated, the Allegany Senecas remained solidly in stage two of the Scudder and Colson model until
at least the early 1970s. The activities of the SNI government emphasized in previous chapters have been those that directly affected
removal, such as housing, and therefore primarily concerned the
people of Allegany. The rehabilitation funds included in House Resolution 1794 were designed to benefit the entire Seneca Nation, reflecting, at least nominally, the recognition that the loss of land and
cultural disruption had ramifications beyond the circle of those directly affected. This has been a source of tension between residents
of the two reservations. Several Allegany people reported having
been chided by Cattaraugus residents for not fighting hard enough
to save their reservation, an idea that unfortunately seems widespread among Allegany youth at the present time. In return, Allegany residents point out that Cattaraugus people received the same
material benefits but without any sacrifice.

At the same time the logistics of removal were being plotted
in the Tribal Council, various committees, composed of council
members and appointed volunteers, were determining the kinds of
projects to be included in section 4, in essence setting the Nation's
course for at least the succeeding decades. These activities placed
the SNI government clearly in the third stage of the model, Community Formation and Economic Development. Prior to 1970 there

were twenty committees and subcommittees dealing with dam-related issues for a total of 114 "positions." These 114 positions were filled by forty-seven Seneca individuals, reflecting the fact that many, in particular the SNI executives, sat on several committees and that all council members sat on at least one, usually as chair. It is possible to isolate a core of approximately twenty individuals who were of major importance because of the duration or extent of their service. Only ten women were committee members, and they were concentrated in the areas of housing (Housing and Relocation Committee, Seneca Nation Housing Authority) and education (Education Committee, Seneca Nation Education Foundation). Seneca women actually outnumbered Seneca men on the latter two committees, but the Education Foundation included white supervisors from the three school districts utilized by Seneca children, thereby giving males a majority.

Seneca planning was not, however, the work of only a handful of politically important individuals. Public meetings and newsletters (especially at Allegany) served to let people know what was under discussion and provided a mechanism for popular expression. A household-by-household survey at Allegany was directed toward ascertaining the residents' priorities for the future. There is no evidence of a similar survey at Cattaraugus; this is understandable since political mobilization was centered at Allegany, and it is likely that Congress would be swayed more by the desires of those it displaced. Nevertheless, council members from Cattaraugus played a major role in planning, and residents of that reservation did mobilize on issues that directly affected them, particularly those relating to industrial development.

EDUCATIONAL PROGRAMS

A primary concern for Allegany Senecas was improved educational opportunities, although, as Fuhriman showed in comparing his survey results with data from the 1960 U.S. census, Senecas under the age of forty compared favorably with non-Indian residents of Cattaraugus County. Of Senecas aged thirty or under, 54.9 percent had completed high school; of those aged thirty-one to forty, 41.2 percent had done so; but only 10.3 percent of those forty-one or over were graduates. Comparable figures for those outside the take area were 48.5 percent, 28 percent, and 15.6 percent, respectively (Fuhriman 1963, 29). Clearly, children born after World War II were better educated than their parents and had great expectations for their own children's educational future. Although the percentage of high school graduates had greatly increased, few Senecas went on to college; there were only two enrolled in the 1961–62 academic year. Enabling students to continue their education at vocational school or college was a goal of the vast majority of Senecas under sixty years of age (38). As previously noted, this was one of the few areas where young people were involved; the Education Committee surveyed all Seneca students in grades seven through twelve on their future goals and plans.

In the spring of 1963, the Kinzua Planning Committee approved in principle the outline of an education program submitted by the Education Committee that called for establishment of a $2.3 million educational trust fund to last for twenty years. The fund was to be administered by a board of trustees from Allegany and Cattaraugus and would utilize the services of professional guidance counselors for the students. This plan was approved by the council in May 1963, and in September 1964 it allocated $1.8 million in section 4 monies to the Seneca Nation Education Foundation. Shortly thereafter it was agreed that interest on the principal would become part of the fund. The following month the certificate of incorporation and by-laws were approved and the first board of trustees appointed. Chaired by Maribel Printup, who had headed the Education Committee, the Education Foundation included the superintendents of the Salamanca Central and Gowanda School Districts for one-year terms, the supervising principal of the Silver Creek Central School for a two-year term, two Seneca men for three-year terms, and two Seneca women for four-year terms.

By March of 1965, before relocation was complete, the foundation was providing aid to fifteen Seneca students pursuing postsecondary education. Not content to merely finance higher education, the foundation moved quickly to ensure that more Seneca children remained in school to benefit from its program. It sponsored summer schools for elementary students requiring or desiring extra help and provided high school students with transportation and tuition for summer school. The foundation supported fifty-two students for the 1965–66 academic year, an incredible increase considering that only two students were enrolled in postsecondary programs four years previously. Recognizing the importance of home-school coordination, in 1969 the foundation hired two special service workers to work with students and their families, the school, and relevant social agencies.

Several factors account for the great success of the Nation's educational effort. First, this was a program actively desired by a majority of the people, including those most directly affected—the young people. Furthermore, unlike other education programs in which the Nation later participated (e.g., Head Start), programs whose broad outlines were set and administered according to policies of the federal government, the Seneca Nation Education Foundation was designed and directed by the people themselves. Second, and probably more important in the long term, the foundation operated outside of Seneca politics. The long, staggered terms of the Seneca trustees ensured that factional disputes within the Nation would not dominate the foundation's decisions. To some extent this reflected the concern of the women, disenfranchised at the time the program was originally proposed to the council, that their input be continued and that education not become a political issue. Many members served multiple terms, thereby ensuring continuity; Merrill Bowen served from the beginning until his death in the spring of 1985, despite the fact that his children, who were not enrolled Senecas, were ineligible for foundation support.

As with any new program, there were difficulties. Some young people viewed foundation sponsorship as a free vacation off the reservation and devoted little time to academic pursuits, eventually losing their scholarships. Initially funding tuition and books, support was soon increased to cover room and board and a small stipend. Another problem was that for many students a college education had seemed an unattainable dream for financial reasons, so some were enrolled in non-college-prep programs or had dropped out. Many students reported that they felt ill-equipped academically to compete with non-Indian students at the integrated high school in Salamanca. Feldsher and Williams (1972, 45) reported that the local opinion was that teachers in the Allegany Indian School were un-

Kinzua Dam, spring 1997. (Photo by Alan LaFlamme)

The old Longhouse at Coldspring, 1964. (Photo courtesy
Marcella Bowen)

Sadie Butler's house on Snow Street in Coldspring, 1964.
(Photo courtesy M. Bowen)

Effie Cornplanter's house at Quaker Bridge, 1964.
(Photo courtesy M. Bowen)

The home of Marcella and Leslie Bowen and their teenage sons, DuWayne ("Duce") and Winfield, in Coldspring, 1965. (Photo courtesy M. Bowen)

"Everyone thinks their home is forever."—Duce Bowen. The remains of the Bowen home, 1965. (Photo courtesy M. Bowen)

(Above left) The relocation
home of the Leslie Bowen
family in Jimersontown, 1965.
(Photo courtesy M. Bowen)

(Left) The old general store and
post office at Quaker Bridge in
the process of demolition prior
to flooding. (Photo courtesy
M. Bowen)

(Above) A relocation home
under construction at
Jimersontown, 1964. (Photo
courtesy M. Bowen)

(Above left) Duce Bowen, 1964.
(Photo courtesy M. Bowen)

(Above) Duce Bowen outside
his home, summer 1997.
(Photo by author)

(Left) George Heron, president
of the sni during removal, who
is still active in community
affairs. (Photo by author)

Mary Moses, an early member
of SWAG, working on the
Nation's newspaper file at the
Allegany branch of the SNI
Library, summer 1997. (Photo
by author)

Harriett Pierce, the Nation's first VISTA volunteer, who is still an active participant in the Area Office on Aging and the SNI Library, summer 1997. (Photo by author)

Seneca-Iroquois National Museum, built with settlement funds from Kinzua Dam. (Photo by author)

First Treaty of North America
THE TWO ROW WAMPUM BELT
KUS-WHEN-TA

This belt symbolizes the agreement and conditions under which th Iroquois welcomed the Europeans to this land. "You say that you are our father and I am your son", "we say we will not be like father and son, but as brothers... as equals." The two rows on this belt will symbolize the paths of two boats on the same river, one path is for the white people, their laws, customs, and their ways, the other path will be for the Onkwehonweh, their laws, customs and way of life. We shall travel side by side but in our own boats, neither of us will try to steer the others vessel, or make laws or interfere in the internal affairs of the other. The Onkwehonweh have kept to this agreement...

HONOR INDIAN

TREATIES RALLY

SUNDAY, APRIL 20TH AT NOON

WE HAVE A GREAT VOICE IN NUMBERS
WELCOMING NATIVE AND NON-NATIVE, TOGETHER
AS NEIGHBORS WE CAN SHOW OUR SUPPORT!

NO VIOLENCE, ALCOHOL OR DRUGS

**THIS IS A PEACEFUL DEMONSTRATION
BRING YOUR SIGNS, BANNERS AND SHIRTS TO SHOW
SUPPORT AGAINST THE GROSS INJUSTICE
TAKING PLACE ON NATIVE TERRITORIES TODAY!**

WHERE: THRUWAY 90 EXIT 58, TO ROUTE 5 & 20
IRVING, NY, CATTARAUGUS BRIDGE

PLENTY OF PARKING AVAILABLE, RESTAURANTS NEARBY
FOR MORE INFORMATION CALL: 1-800-439-6899 OR 1-800-336-4220

Poster announcing rally during 1997 taxation dispute with New York State. (Photo by author)

Seneca Nation Council member
Richard Jemison and unidentified
New York state trooper at tax
demonstration on New York
Thruway (Interstate 90), 13 April
1997. (Photo by Sandy Jemison)

suitable for employment in the Salamanca schools. Whether this was true is unclear; nevertheless, it was a perception shared by numerous students. Feelings of academic inferiority and social awkwardness hampered the learning of Seneca students, a problem the foundation tried to address by making school administrators more sensitive to Seneca concerns. By the early 1970s the Nation, via a Community Action Program in conjunction with the principal and teachers from the Seneca Elementary School, had begun a class for parents of preschool children to familiarize them with school policies, procedures, and personnel in order to avoid later problems and involve parents more directly in their children's education.

As students began to stay in school longer, local school districts on both reservations benefited from increased Indian enrollment in the form of additional subsidies for special programs as well as government payments to the districts in lieu of Seneca property taxes. Widespread charges of discrimination against Seneca students in one school district in the 1970s forced Robert Hoag, the SNI president, to remind school administrators of this fact and threaten removal of Seneca children to another district. Hoag's threat was preceded by Indian school boycotts at Onondaga and Akwesasne, although Hoag himself did not mention these as prompting his action. His threat can be seen as successful in that problems abated rapidly. (Other boycotts were undertaken in the 1990s as a result of anti-Seneca attitudes connected to the Salamanca lease dispute and over the taxation issue.) The schools benefited in another way as well. Seneca students, particularly boys, were often outstanding athletes, bringing renown not only to themselves but also to their school. One former student recalled that this was a mixed blessing. Comparing himself with a sibling who was not a school athlete, he stated that the sibling received much more attention and encouragement from teachers, whereas as long as he was athletically successful the faculty was unconcerned with his academic progress. He felt this pattern was true for all Seneca students. Although this comment was received too late in the research to test it adequately, widespread reports of nearly illiterate non-Indian athletes in the popular media suggest that differential treatment of athletes is widespread.

Students in Salamanca schools were also confronted with a lack of role models in the school system because there were no Indian teachers or administrators. A number of students reported that they missed the more personal relationship they had with teachers at the Allegany Indian School and felt that some teachers in Salamanca schools disliked Indian students. While reports of discrimination are too widespread to be without foundation, Seneca students already traumatized to some extent by removal may well have been more sensitive to the changes implicit in a shift to a more impersonal high school environment. An undercurrent of tension seems to have existed between Indian and non-Indian students. High school yearbooks of Indian students often had messages from non-Indian peers such as "To a good Injun" or "Have fun this summer in teepee town." While the owners of the yearbooks usually dismissed these with comments such as, "Oh, he didn't really mean that" or "We always used to talk that way," the inherent racism in the messages is apparent to outside observers; that it was not recognized as such at the time is probably indicative of fairly pervasive institutional discrimination. That many older Senecas were willing participants in this is indicated by statements like, "We were just dumb Indians" despite the fact that the entire removal experience provided definitive proof to the contrary. Regardless of the potential handicaps of this tension and racism, the success of the Seneca Nation Education Foundation reflects the determination of the Seneca Nation and that of non-Seneca teachers and administrators who shared the Nation's goal.

ECONOMIC AND COMMUNITY DEVELOPMENT

The factors most responsible for the success of the educational program—strong popular support and removal of administration from the political arena—did not operate in the Nation's plans for industrial development and partly explain its relative lack of success. To a significant extent this was inevitable; development, particularly that relating to industry, requires decisions on the allocation of land and resources that are not easily revocable, and this necessitates political choices. Although there was general agreement on the need to provide employment for Senecas, consensus dissolved over the particulars. Because proposals by various corporations for plant construction on Nation land became the focus of factional politics and extended debate, many companies decided to look elsewhere. The biennial election of the executive branch may have been interpreted as political instability by industries used to dealing with political leaders with longer terms of office. While the Education Committee and its successor, the Seneca Nation Education Foundation, were relatively independent of the Tribal Council, the specifics of any recommendation of the Industrial Development Committee had to be considered by the council. In less stressful times it would have been able to sort through proposals more rapidly, although not necessarily more effectively, but it must be remembered that because the SNI government was at this time concerned with the relocation at Allegany, industrial development was definitely of secondary importance.

Those attending the first meeting of the Economic Development and Employment Subcommittee of the Kinzua Planning Committee in January 1963 were primarily concerned that Senecas would be employed in the construction of relocation housing. The separate Industrial Development Committee was not formed until November, a month after the Fruit of the Loom Corporation inquired about locating on the reservations. At this time the council authorized a survey to ascertain the number of employable women available, a concern apparently raised by Fruit of the Loom, which foresaw hiring a maximum of 250. Upon finding an adequate number of women, the Nation, represented by George Heron and Sidney Carney, met with company representatives in New York City, and both the Nation and the BIA considered the possibility of a Fruit of the Loom factory, although no action was taken. At this time the BIA assigned a social science analyst to aid the Nation in preparing a program for the Area Redevelopment Administration, which suggested that the required submission of an Overall Economic Development Program should be made in two months. To expect this of the Nation, still without any idea of the extent of government compensation available and without suitable housing for its relocatees, was patently absurd. Compounding this situation was the fact that the Nation was still nearly three years away from formulating its first budget and setting up a bookkeeping system.

By March 1965 nine firms had expressed interest in relocating to Seneca property, six had been inspected by the Nation, and two were invited to submit proposals, one of which was deemed suitable for further negotiation. It should be noted that industrial development would necessarily be located on the Cattaraugus Reservation since there was little, if any, suitable land available at Allegany. By April 1965 the Tribal Council identified two sites in the Irving area, bounded by Route 5 and the New York Central Railroad tracks, as industrial development sites. Negotiations with the U.S. Pillow Corporation occurred during the summer, and in the fall the council endorsed an agreement with the corporation to establish a new company, the First Seneca Corporation, on Cattaraugus, voting to spend $800,000 on the project. Ground was broken for the new Industrial Park, which was financed by a $297,000 grant from the federal Economic Development Agency, in May 1966 by BIA Commissioner Robert Bennett, but the project was troubled from the beginning. In February the contractor defaulted. Senator Robert F. Kennedy (D-NY) dedicated the First Seneca plant in July; within five years the corporation was liquidated, never having employed a significant number of Senecas and leaving the Nation with a vacant building in January 1972.

Advised by their attorney and the BIA, the Nation cannot be seen as solely responsible for what in retrospect was a bad investment. Indeed, to this day Senecas knowledgeable about the negotiations with U.S. Pillow express amazement at the outcome, stressing that a thorough investigation of the company's finances revealed no indication of problems. It is clear from the number of proposals received and the number actually seriously considered that the Nation was not blindly seeking any development project. However, by the time First Seneca failed, there were those, especially at Cattaraugus, who were beginning to question the whole idea of industrial development, and their opposition, in the council and the court system, doomed the best opportunity for successful development presented to the Seneca Nation.

As the demise of the pillow factory became apparent, the Fisher-Price Company, a manufacturer of children's toys, expressed interest in acquiring space in the Industrial Park. The council, by a vote of fourteen to zero, approved. Opposition to Fisher-Price was centered in the new Seneca Constitutional Rights Organization, composed primarily of Cattaraugus residents who stated that they were opposed to any further loss of Seneca land and that they did not want what happened at Allegany to happen at Cattaraugus, even though the situations were not comparable. Their attorney, Omar Ghobashy, who had documented the Tuscaroras' fight against the New York Power Authority (Ghobashy 1961), filed suit in federal court in Buffalo to prevent Fisher-Price from locating at Cattaraugus, arguing that the SNI Council was illegal because of vote buying. In August the Economic Development Agency approved federal grants for the Fisher-Price project, and the dissidents' lawsuit was dismissed from district court, although this was appealed to the Second Circuit Court of Appeals. Strong support for the Fisher-Price project was apparent at Allegany, where the editor of *Oh-He-Yoh-Noh* published instructions concerning how proponents both on and off the reservation could organize to ensure the company would come to Cattaraugus. It can be argued that on this issue people at Allegany had nothing to lose.

There is another reason why Allegany residents might have looked more favorably on industrial development. By this time most of the relocatees had been in their new homes for over six years and were becoming used to suburban living, particularly at Jimersontown, where residents were within walking distance of employment opportunities. Relocation had served to create important differences between the two reservations. In the words of one Cattaraugus resident in the mid 1980s, "Going to Allegany from Cattaraugus is like going to the city." The essentially rural life that Allegany residents had fought so hard to retain was still the pattern at Cattaraugus, and many people there wanted to make sure it remained that way. At any rate, the specter of court fights and strong minority opposition led Fisher-Price to lose interest in the idea. Given the financial success of the company, hindsight clearly shows that if some accommodation had been possible between the two factions that would have permitted Fisher-Price to locate in the Industrial Park, the Nation would have benefited significantly in terms of employment and income.

Another development project, this time focused on recreation, was also unsuccessful and was finally stopped in 1975 after the estimated expenditure of at least $1 million. Recreational development was widely touted at the time the dam was proposed, and the Nation sought advice from various state and federal agencies as how best to exploit the recreational potential of the reservoir. The area most often cited as best for development was Hotchkiss Hollow, near the area known as Highbanks. In January 1963 the Nation contracted with Brill Engineering to develop a plan that could be inserted in section 4 of H.R. 1794. In June the Tribal Council approved Brill's suggestion of a $29 million recreational area to be known as Iroquoia and modeled after Williamsburg, Virginia. It called for the impoundment of Hotchkiss Run, with the resulting formation of an artificial lake, similar to Red House Lake in Allegany State Park several miles away. Aside from the obvious recreational potential of the lake, the plans for Iroquoia included the use of Hotchkiss plateau to the northeast for a reconstructed Iroquois village as a kind of living museum, providing an accurate antidote to Hollywood images of marauding Iroquois scalping innocent women and children. Iroquoia would be directed and staffed by Indian people and would provide cultural education as well as jobs for young Senecas. Tourist facilities such as a motel and campground would also be provided. The scope of the plans for Iroquoia caught the imagination of many people at Allegany, in part because these plans represented a living image of Seneca ethnicity at a time when the people were attempting to reestablish themselves as Senecas in a new environment. Iroquoia was perhaps the logical theoretical outcome of a period of cultural involution, representing a strong statement of the underlying conservatism of Iroquoian people but blended with a pragmatic recognition of twentieth-century economic reality.

What is surprising, therefore, is that the Provisional Planning Committee for Iroquoia was the only relocation committee on which Senecas were not a majority. As noted, the education committees included white educators, and Walt Taylor and Sid Carney sat on several other committees whose other members were all Senecas. The Iroquoia committee, temporarily chaired by William Fenton, also included Arthur Lazarus, then the Nation's attorney, Carney, Taylor, and four Senecas. With no intended cynicism it is possible to understand the enthusiasm of the non-Senecas as well. For Fenton, participation in the tangible reconstruction of a culture he had dedicated a lifetime to documenting would be a crowning professional achievement. Yet it would be unfair to imply that Fenton's motives were purely or even primarily professional. His wife, Olive, was a native of Salamanca who had many close Seneca friends, and both she and her husband were personally affected by what was happening to them. The financial rewards for the attorney representing the Seneca Nation in a $29 million project are obvious. Similar grandiose plans by tribes dislocated by the Pick-Sloan Plan had resulted in failure. If Carney could help make the Seneca attempt successful, he would succeed where others had failed. The mutual affection between the Allegany Senecas and Walt and Peggy Taylor is as deep as it is obvious. Clearly Iroquoia would have been as emotionally satisfying to Taylor as it was to the Senecas.

In order to make Iroquoia a reality, the Seneca Nation purchased nearly five hundred acres of Hotchkiss Hollow but in doing so committed several costly errors. First, the Nation neglected to acquire subsurface rights, which remained with the seller, in an area where sand and gravel resources should be found. Second, it did not seek reservation status for the new land, thereby making it liable to taxation. Both these situations can be remedied, although the first may be costly and would probably not be justified until such time as the Nation decides to develop the area. Obtaining reservation status requires congressional action; it is not clear if this can be achieved prior to extinguishing subsurface rights.

Hindsight again suggests that construction of Iroquoia as originally conceived would have committed the Nation to a project with virtually no chance of recouping even a small portion of its investment in the foreseeable future. Although the situation was somewhat better twenty years ago, the area today is severely depressed economically. Non-Indian residents of Salamanca tend to point to the lease question as a major cause, but this is obviously a minor element. General economic conditions in the entire area of southwestern New York and northwestern Pennsylvania are bleak, and the decline of the railroads, the reason for the original development of Salamanca, is the major local cause of economic depression.

Portions of the Iroquoia concept have in fact become reality. A small but impressive museum, including a reconstructed longhouse as well as examples of contemporary Iroquois art, was built in the mid 1970s in Salamanca near Jimersontown and today provides jobs as guides for young Senecas. The area adjacent to Hotchkiss Hollow has been made into Highbanks Campground, which has cabins as well as electric sites for those who enjoy camping with all the amenities of home and heavily wooded nonelectric sites for those desiring a more rustic experience where a chance meeting with a black bear or deer occasionally occurs. Should economic conditions change, it could provide tourist residences for a revived Iroquoia.

Some local whites as well as some Indians point to the spotty record of the Nation's exploits in development as proof that Indians lack "good business sense" or that Seneca cultural values preclude business success in a capitalist society. While value differences do in fact exist, a more accurate assessment would explain the problems in terms of Seneca priorities in the decade following removal. That Senecas can be extremely successful in the white business world is shown by Barry Snyder at Cattaraugus and Maurice "Moe" John and Robert Hoag at Allegany.

Besides building for development, the Senecas also developed resources for their own use. In early 1963 the Tribal Council applied to the Housing and Home Finance Agency for aid in the financing and construction of tribal offices and community buildings on each reservation. The office building at Allegany, named the Haley Building in honor of Congressman Haley, was dedicated in May 1966. A similar building at Cattaraugus was named after Representative John Saylor (R-PA), the sole member of the Pennsylvania congressional delegation to oppose Kinzua Dam. Although both reservations had government offices, the Nation's daily administration tended to concentrate at the Haley Building in Jimersontown. By the mid 1980s this distinction was very apparent. Of thirty SNI departments or bureaus, fourteen were located at Allegany, five were at Cattaraugus, and eleven had offices on both reservations. While this does not mean that services provided by a department are exclusively available at the reservation where it is headquartered, it does indicate where employment opportunities are concentrated.

In addition to emphasizing differences between Allegany and Cattaraugus, this concentration at Jimersontown further distinguished the two relocation communities. The only Allegany departments located at Steamburg were Head Start, the Health Clinic, and Bingo, but by 1987 Bingo was moved to Salamanca, despite concerns by non-Indian organizations that high-stakes games would significantly cut into the revenues generated by their own games. Community buildings for recreational purposes were completed in the early 1970s at both Jimersontown and Steamburg, but activities tended to be centered at the former because it had the swimming pool and was the location of the summer recreation program. Bus or van transportation was provided for children living in Steamburg, but for obvious reasons they were unable to utilize the facilities as fully as those living in Jimersontown. Furthermore, the Steamburg community building also served as the cookhouse for the Coldspring Longhouse.

At the same time the SNI government was planning and executing removal and drawing up plans for development, it was called upon to again defend the integrity of the Nation's land base. Although Public Law 88–533 called for the Nation to submit to Congress a plan for termination of federal responsibility, the people had been told that termination would not occur without a favorable referendum vote; most, busy with the problems of removal, did not consider termination a serious threat.

THREATS OF TERMINATION AND HIGHWAY EXPANSION

Section 18 of the Kinzua Dam Act called for a termination plan to be submitted prior to 31 August 1967. Seneca officials met with representatives of the BIA and various congresspeople in the beginning of the year, and the council sent two members to Washington to report on the hearings on termination. BIA Commissioner Robert Bennett came to the Special Session of the council at Allegany on 31 July 1967, at which time the Senecas expected him to present a plan for termination of federal supervision. Instead, he called for the Nation to submit a plan, suggesting only a few items for inclusion. He once again assured the Senecas that any termination bill would include a tribal referendum on the issue and noted that since 1957 no termination had occurred without a tribal vote. Having just learned how readily Congress could put aside a treaty, Senecas responded with justifiable wariness if not outright skepticism. Once again the Quakers and Arthur Morgan volunteered their help in case of a congressional fight. More surprising is that for the first time the Faith-keepers of the Longhouse, who, as a body, had taken no public ac-tion against the dam, now took a strong stand against termination in a letter to Interior Secretary Stewart Udall, which they sub-mitted to SNI president Calvin "Kelly" John for forwarding. The council authorized John to add his signature as president to the Faithkeepers' letter, in which six Faithkeepers from the Newtown Longhouse at Cattaraugus and five from the Coldspring Longhouse at Allegany concluded, "And now, as to the lands that remain to us, our plea is that the United States Government abide by its part in the provisions agreed upon under articles one and three of the Treaty of 1794—grant us the peace that is so badly needed in these troubled days and permit us to occupy our lands without further molestation or disturbance." Senate bill 2390, introduced by Sena-tor Henry "Scoop" Jackson (D-WA) and strongly promoted by Sena-tor Clinton Anderson (D-NM), called for termination of the Senecas but died in committee.

The other threat to Seneca land was also related directly to Kin-zua Dam. In June 1962 the Corps of Engineers told the Senecas, then searching for appropriate sites for relocation areas, to avoid areas that might be utilized for a four-lane highway planned as a replace-ment for the old two-lane Route 17, which lay within the take area, and the Tribal Council announced it might oppose this collabora-tion between the corps and the state of New York. In January 1963 the Nation announced its willingness to negotiate on a two-lane Route 17 but not on four lanes. When it granted a right of entry to the federal government to effect the alteration or relocation of state roads within the reservation, it made approval exclusive of Route 17. Over Seneca objections, the corps agreed to condemn an ease-ment for the road across Nation land at the same time that it con-demned land for the take area. Arthur Lazarus argued for the Nation that the Treaty of 1794 protected the land being condemned for the highway, and the judge asked the government to prove it needed a four-lane highway at that time. In January 1964 Judge Henderson upheld the federal condemnation for a four-lane highway but gave the Nation the right to an immediate appeal. The Federal Appeals Court upheld Henderson's decision by a two to one vote, with the majority decision written by Thurgood Marshall. In his lone dissent, Judge Leonard Moore stated that the expansion of Route 17 was a project independent of the dam and that Congress should decide whether or not to give New York State authority to take the land. A 31 October editorial in the *New York Times* expressed support for Moore's position. The council immediately authorized Lazarus to appeal to the Supreme Court, an appeal that was unsuccessful.

ADJUSTMENT TO RELOCATION

By the mid 1970s the residents of Steamburg and Jimersontown had begun to feel at home in the new communities and had initiated the process of risk taking indicative of stage three in the Scudder and Colson model, Community Formation and Economic Development. This is apparent from *Oh-He-Yoh-Noh*, in which nostalgic articles about the old places and ways, common in the decade following removal, gave way to articles about activities and projects in the relocation sites. This change in attitude is best exemplified by a poem by the late Nellie Jack that appeared in the 28 November 1978 issue.

Jimersontown

I like to live in Jimersontown
Where the Haley Building is across the road,
And where the beautiful trees are around,
Where you wave your hand and say, "Hi,"
To everyone you meet.
I like to stand for a moment outside my place,
And listen to friendly gossip
Of the folks that live around Jimersontown.

Absolutely life is interwoven
With the friends I learn to know,
And I hear their joys and sorrows,
As I daily come and go.
So I like to live in Jimersontown,
I care no more to roam,
For every house in Jimersontown,
Is more than a house—it's home.

This change is also confirmed by the disappearance of most of the organizations that arose in the dam era and provided focal points for reorganized social interaction. The exception to this was the Seniors, which continued to flourish, organizing bus trips to the Canadian National Exposition and the Grand Ole Opry.

The convergence of a number of trends, not all related to Kinzua, resulted in the enhanced cultural awareness and a "can do" spirit that typified the Seneca Nation and people by this time. Feeling more at ease in the new communities played a major role that was facilitated by a number of community programs, often funded through the Community Action Program (CAP) and later the Community Action Agency, which encouraged the participation of large numbers of people in projects whose benefits were readily apparent. Harriett Pierce became the Nation's first VISTA volunteer at this time. These projects also provided experience in leadership and management for young adults, particularly women, for whom access to positions of political importance was still limited. Many who would later move into the political arena received their first training in public service in CAP activities such as legal aid, tax assistance, on-the-job training, and cultural enrichment programs. In addition to valuable experience for the individuals involved, these programs also provided a focal point for increased community pride. Utilizing funds available from the federal government, they did not seriously affect the Nation's financial stability and allowed people to confront and attempt to solve community problems.

Outsiders pointed to a strong SNI program to combat alcoholism that was developed at this time as indicative of increased substance abuse problems. Whether the problem had increased in severity or extent is not apparent, but certainly public awareness was heightened. Some Senecas attribute this awareness to the change in housing, claiming that in the relocation sites more people were aware of drunken behavior because of the proximity of the houses. Others, those involved in alcohol-related programs, discount this, claiming that even in the old places people knew who the drunks were. Nevertheless, it is obvious that in the new communities those who drank were more likely to come into contact with neighbors, and the effects of the behavior had wider social impact. Community role models were also important in confronting the problem. Most prominent among these was Inez Redeye, whose willingness to openly admit her alcoholism and seek treatment, including hospitalization, helped bring the subject into the open. As a recovered alcoholic, she became a trained counselor and briefly headed the Alcoholism Counseling Program. After over a decade of sobriety, she still informally counseled alcoholics and their families until ill health, not related to past alcohol abuse, made her give up this activity.

Heightened cultural awareness was reflected by increased interest in traditional arts and crafts and formation of the Seneca Nation Organization for the Visual Arts in 1974. Classes in beadwork, dance, and cornhusk doll making were common; overall, however, removal had a negative effect on craft production. Avery Jimerson, the preeminent Seneca mask carver, never made another mask after relocation. Pounding ash for basket splints became rare since many of the ash trees were in the take area and as those who knew how to make splints became too old to do so. By the mid 1980s only three generations of the Watt family made the traditional baskets, and they got most of the splints from another reservation. Unlike the Mohawks, the Senecas use no wooden form to shape their baskets, which are in great demand by museums. During the summer of 1985 Nettie Watt was busy trying to fill an order for twenty-five baskets from the Cleveland Museum of Natural History prior to leaving for Washington DC to demonstrate the art of basket making at the annual Smithsonian Folklife Festival. The Seneca Iroquois National Museum, by sponsoring "Living Artists" series during the summer months, provided a means for artisans to demonstrate their skills for both tourists and would-be Seneca apprentices. Crafts, particularly beadwork, provide a source of extra income for many artists and the museum and several Indian-owned shops serve as retail outlets.

Concern with ethnic heritage became more pronounced in the mid 1970s. The Iroquois Archaeological Society was founded in 1973 to inform people about the role of archaeologists in preserving evidence of former ways of life and to provide training for Senecas interested in working on an archaeological dig. This coincided with excavations on the reservation, interest in which was high since the Iroquoia concept was still being seriously considered. Unfortunately, some of the excavations were directed by a man whose only aca-

demic degree was an honorary Ph.D. from a small school with no
anthropology program and produced artifacts whose location is currently unknown by staff of the Seneca Iroquois National Museum.
Whether his credentials were purposefully misrepresented or just
misunderstood by the Senecas cannot be ascertained, but the long-
term effects include a legacy of hostility toward anthropologists,
particularly archaeologists, at Allegany. The Nation was successful
at this time in recovering three wampum belts offered for public
sale in New York City. The Tribal Council authorized President
Calvin John to purchase the belts, and the private seller agreed to
donate an additional one. These are now on display at the museum.

Seneca pride was also enhanced by the wave of Indian activism,
often referred to as Red Power, that was prevalent throughout the
country at this time. Seneca young people, still angry about Kinzua,
had gone off to college, ironically because of Kinzua, where they
came into contact with other Indians and became involved in college as well as national Indian organizations, including the American Indian Movement (AIM). At the same time, younger Senecas in
the high school formed the Seneca Indian Youth Council, and
Americans for Indian Opportunity (AIO) founded a chapter there. To
some older, more politically conservative Senecas, the latter organization was viewed as dangerously leftist and rabble-rousing, a
viewpoint held strongly by the editor of *Oh-He-Yoh-Noh*. After a
particularly harsh attack on the AIO, one of its teenage leaders,
Becki Bowen, courageously sought a meeting with the editor, at
which time she presented the organization's goals and ideas. The
success of her overture was apparent in the next issue, in which
Bowen was praised as a thoughtful and intelligent young woman
and the organization was depicted in a different light. These organizations were especially important in providing a common focus for
Seneca students in the high school, allowing them to demonstrate
ethnic pride in an appropriate educational context. At this time participation by Indian students increased in other areas as well. In the
early 1970s the few participating in nonathletic school-sponsored
activities tended to be concentrated in areas like distributive education. By the middle of the decade there had been a shift to more
professional and academic areas such as Future Nurses and French
Club.

In comparison with other New York Iroquois, particularly the Onondagas and Mohawks, the Seneca Nation has been perceived as quite conservative. Outside political "agitators" have never been welcome, even at the height of the Red Power movement. Yet the increased political activism of the young people was not without support. Diane Rothenberg, an anthropologist living at Allegany in the 1970s, described watching elders view television coverage of the AIM takeover at Wounded Knee (1986a). Although they uniformly decried the methods and tactics used, their pleasure at seeing the Indians hold off the U.S. government was undisguised. Concern with propriety and decorum is paramount with older Senecas but should not be confused with political conservatism. Disgust with some of the actions taken by "radicals" coexists with agreement on goals.

The formation of the new People's Party expressed this new attitude of self-confidence. It swept into power in 1974, winning every elected position. With this election, the Allegany Senecas joined their government in stage three of the Scudder-Colson model, Community Formation and Economic Development. Heading the ticket was the newly elected president, Robert Hoag of Allegany. Born into a politically powerful family (his grandfather had been president for many years in the nineteenth century, and another relative, Willie Hoag, had been president as recently as 1927), he was raised on the reservation but was sent by his parents to schools in Salamanca. Married to a white woman and living in the city, Hoag was not relocated, although his first experience in Seneca government occurred during the Kinzua era when he was a member of the Economic Development and Employment Subcommittee. In December 1965 he was appointed to fill an unexpired term on the Tribal Council. Although the Hoags were large landowners and therefore relatively affluent, Robert Hoag's specific economic focus was a construction company he founded in Salamanca as well as sand and gravel interests from reservation property.

Hoag was certainly the pivotal figure of the post-Kinzua era, and few people are ambivalent toward him. To his supporters, he was a charismatic leader who made things happen, a man with vision. In the words of one admirer, "Look at the Nation. When Hoag's in charge, things work; when he isn't, they fall apart." To his opponents, he personified development and the adoption of white values. He was seen as the person most responsible for federal government programs, a man whose personal wealth was gained at the Nation's expense and whose primary loyalty was to Salamanca.

It was not just the election of Bob Hoag that signaled the entry into stage three. The 1974 election also marked a new phase in Seneca politics, foreshadowed in the previous election, in which issues and expertise were more important than family alliances. A number of other individuals also began their rise to prominence in this election, including Maurice "Moe" John, a relocatee and air force veteran who had returned to Allegany and was just beginning his career as a successful businessman. Although he worked with Hoag during his term on the council, by the mid 1980s they had become bitter political rivals, running against each other for the presidency in 1986.

The dominance of the People's Party ushered in a period of increased government efficiency and accountability. The monthly newsletter now included detailed accounts of funds expended and their sources. Young people were brought into government service as the Nation began to take advantage of the large number of college students and graduates.

In terms of development, the Nation finally discarded Iroquoia as a viable project, moving instead to less audacious programs more likely to produce profits. The first of these was Highbanks Campground, which opened in June 1975 at a total cost of eight hundred thousand dollars, of which the SNI contribution was one hundred thousand dollars from section 4 funds. A bowling alley, built on part of twenty-two acres purchased in the west end of Salamanca, generated seven hundred dollars a day by the fall of 1975, despite managerial problems. By the end of the year, plans for a museum adjacent to the bowling alley had been approved for full funding by the Economic Development Agency. Operating costs for the Seneca Iroquois National Museum, which opened in 1977, were supplemented by annual grants from the New York State Council on the Arts. The museum's failure to generate profits has angered many who do not realize that most museums are not self-supporting. Because there was no admission charge, the only income generated by the museum came from the sale of Indian-made crafts and books and voluntary contributions by visitors. This was changed in 1996 when admission fees were charged for non-Indians. The final building on the purchased land was the Allegany branch of the Seneca Nation Library. A library was also constructed at Cattaraugus.

As more people were employed by the Nation (165 by June 1975), many of them women, a day-care center was developed for the children of parents employed full-time. Concern was also expressed for elders who might be unable to care for themselves in their relocation homes or to move in with adult children. Plans for a housing complex for the elderly at one of the relocation sites was stymied by the lack of land. Therefore, in 1976 the Nation began to explore the idea of a joint effort with the city of Salamanca, which had land but no funds. A joint project was eventually approved and constructed. Because many of the newly created jobs went to younger Senecas due to their higher education levels, elders were at a slight economic disadvantage. Traditional roles of helping to care for grandchildren were not available to those who did not relocate to the same community as their children, who had no means of transportation, or whose children lived off the reservation. To provide activities as well as income for these people, the Nation sought and received a forty-four-thousand-dollar grant from the New York State Office of Aging to employ ten seniors in Nation programs. Elders worked in various jobs such as library aides and "grandmothers" in preschool programs.

The Indian Education Act made available additional programs including adult education in preparation for the GED examination and bilingual and bicultural programs in the local schools. The first Indian culture courses were taught in the Salamanca schools in 1976. The Education Foundation took responsibility for several of these, including job counseling (an obvious parallel to the Career Days it sponsored for high school students), and the Johnson-O'Malley Act supported counseling and tutorial programs.

Volunteer fire departments were started at both Cattaraugus and Allegany. The Allegany Indian Reservation Volunteer Fire Department (AIRVFD) was located in Jimersontown and provided protection for that community as well as additional backup support for the city of Salamanca. Although predominantly Indian, there were white members as well. Fire protection for Steamburg was provided by the Coldspring Volunteer Fire Department in the village of Steamburg, a primarily white force. The Cattaraugus department initiated bingo games in 1975 in an attempt to be self-supporting. A Fall Festival at Allegany, modeled after one at Cattaraugus, was started in 1976 as a means of uniting and celebrating the reservation. This also attracted non-Indian visitors, thereby opening further lines of contact with surrounding white communities.

SETTLEMENT FOR ROUTE 17

The most controversial action taken by the Seneca Nation in the 1970s was the agreement with New York State for the construction of the uncompleted sixteen-mile segment of Route 17, the Southern Tier Expressway, through the Allegany Reservation from Salamanca to Vandalia. Over Seneca objections, the federal courts had permitted the Corps of Engineers to condemn land for the highway between Steamburg and Salamanca. This land had been taken as an easement and compensation was paid to individual landowners. Failing to justify the highway on grounds of use or strategic importance, the New York Department of Transportation cited its usefulness in promoting regional economic development (Hauptman 1986b, 166). Many Senecas in the mid 1970s saw the completion of Route 17 as an incentive to business, which would be drawn by improved transportation to locate on or near the reservation and thus provide job opportunities for unemployed individuals. Additionally, it was believed that increased tourist traffic on the new road would benefit Seneca recreational facilities. Others, however, were opposed to any further loss of land.

In early 1972 the Department of Transportation indicated it would not continue the project without an agreement with the Seneca Nation. Theoretically this raised the possibility of the return of some of the land condemned by the dam since it was to revert to the Nation in the event that it was not used for its intended purpose. The record of New York State dealings with Indians indicates, however, that this was extremely unlikely (Hauptman 1986b). Both state officials and the more development-minded segments of the Seneca population desired the highway, and in July 1976 the Nation and New York signed an Agreement of Adjustment and Memorandum of Understanding permitting the construction of the final segment of the Southern Tier Expressway.

The Agreement of Adjustment provided an easement on 795 acres of Seneca land for the highway to New York State and compensation for the Nation in the amount of $494,386 (plus 6 percent interest since 1972) and shares of $1,303,858 to be divided among the landowners based on amount of land taken. In addition, the Nation received 795 acres of lieu lands, derived primarily from Allegany State Park. Signed at the same time was a Memorandum of Understanding that called for the Department of Transportation to construct and maintain access roads to the lieu lands as well as the maintenance of specified roads within each reservation. The department also agreed to support, "to the maximum extent feasible," Seneca proposals for improved health care, transportation on the reservations, industrial development, and exemptions for its members from state game laws. The Tribal Council passed the Agreement of Adjustment and Memorandum of Understanding by a vote of twelve to zero with four abstentions. A key provision of the agreement was paragraph 8, in which the Nation agreed to the application of section 30 of the New York State Highway Law on the reservation, thereby allowing the state to use eminent domain to acquire the interests of individual landowners unable or unwilling to reach an agreement with the state.

The signing of both documents was a major ceremonial occasion. Various state, local, and Seneca Nation politicians spoke briefly. New York Transportation Commissioner Raymond Schuler presented the Nation with two movie screens for use in classrooms; Raymond Harding, special assistant to Governor Hugh Carey, presented President Hoag with a letter of congratulations from the governor, and Councilor Maurice John presented a red, white, and blue tie to Harding. William T. Hennessy, the major negotiator for the state, was adopted into the Beaver Clan. Lost in the pomp was the prescient question posed by Councilor Cornelius Abrams Jr.: "how long would this instrument stay alive if the environmentalists or our traditionalists objected to the construction of the Expressway?" Sidestepping the question, Hennessy responded that the agreement would survive a change in administration. The answer to the question did not become apparent until the summer of 1985 and is examined in the following chapter.

An interesting footnote to the negotiations between the Seneca Nation and the state of New York is provided by Laurence Hauptman, who suggests that the form of the final document was influenced by state concerns over the Oneida land claims case, in which New York argued that federal oversight was not required in its dealings with Indian nations. In order not to counter its own argument, a provision in the Agreement of Adjustment for approval by the secretary of the interior was deleted, and the sole signatories were President Robert Hoag, Clerk Genevieve Plummer, and Treasurer Calvin Lay for the Nation and Commissioner Raymond Schuler and Gerald Hall of the Department of Audit and Control for New York (Hauptman 1986b, 170–78).

SIX

The 1980s: Rebellion and Reassessment

By the mid 1980s it was apparent that the Allegany Reservation had changed radically in the two decades following removal. The communities along the river were replaced by two increasingly different settlements. Jimersontown, with the fire hall, day-care center, Montessori school, swimming pool, Nautilus facility, and SNI government buildings, was clearly the social and economic hub of the reservation. Nearby, although within the city limits of Salamanca, was the Seneca-Iroquois National Museum, Seneca Lanes bowling alley, the Allegany branch of the SNI Library, the Seneca Mini-Mart and gas station, an Indian-owned restaurant serving an Indian food buffet on Wednesday nights, and two Indian-owned craft shops. Its more suburban character was also reflected by more violence and crime, frequently centered on an after-hours bottle club.

Twelve miles away, via the four-lane, limited-access Southern Tier Expressway (Route 17), was Steamburg. Decidedly more rural, only Head Start, the health clinic, and bingo were located there. In the summer of 1985 the Nation decided to explore the possibility of building a clinic in Jimersontown, retaining the Steamburg location only as a satellite facility. This latter plan was dropped, and in 1993 the newly constructed Lionel R. John Health Center opened in Jimersontown, the only health facility at Allegany. Along the same lines, in the summer of 1987 the Nation moved its bingo operation from its community building and cookhouse in Steamburg to the former Seneca Lanes bowling alley in Salamanca, a move that provoked opposition in both the Nation and the city. Salamanca officials were concerned over the negative impact Seneca bingo might have on local churches and interest groups that depended on income from small games. Ironically, the Senecas I knew best who played bingo played at a local church and the Salamanca VFW post because it was cheaper. Unlike many of the whites who played in hopes of winning big, the Senecas played for fun.

There is no public transportation between the two sites, and Steamburg residents still have to go into the village to pick up their mail at the post office. Until the spring of 1995 phone calls between Steamburg and Jimersontown were billed as "long distance," and the communities' phone listings were contained in two different directories. The Seneca Nation tried to ease this problem by publishing a reservation phone book, a project that dates to the time of removal.

Although the source of the differences between Steamburg and Jimersontown is frequently attributed to the conservative influence of the Coldspring Longhouse at Steamburg, other reasons are as likely. The proximity of Salamanca to Jimersontown makes the location of income-producing projects in Jimersontown logical from an economic perspective. Furthermore, the continuing drainage problems at Steamburg make building for development precarious. A test of the Longhouse hypothesis will occur when the leaders, many of whom live in Steamburg, pass away and younger, possibly non-Longhouse, families move into their homes. It is highly unlikely, however, that the differences between the two reservations will diminish since there seems to be a strong trend in the opposite direction that will not be easily reversed. The most probable cause for reversal would be if the Nation decided to move toward full-scale recreational development in the Highbanks–Hotchkiss Hollow area in the future.

EMPLOYMENT

The most obvious changes in the Seneca Nation have been in the area of government expansion. Twenty years after the Nation hired George Heron as its first ever full-time employee, it was employing nearly four hundred individuals on both reservations and was the major employer at Allegany. While the expansion of SNI jobs has provided a necessary safety net for Senecas as jobs in Salamanca disappeared due to the demise or relocation of industries there, many see this as a mixed blessing. The People's Party refused to expend SNI funds on any project that could be provided by the state or federal governments, thus preserving the interest-bearing section 4 monies. The effect of this choice was that many of the jobs (up to a third by some estimates) on the reservation were dependent on outside funding, much of which could be withdrawn. The Hoag administration (1988–90) vowed to reduce this dependence on outside sources of support by making the Nation more self-sufficient. Along with many other Indian nations, the Senecas discovered that the income from high-stakes bingo games could be used to offset the cutbacks in federal funding imposed by the Reagan administration. Unlike the highly publicized and often violent altercations caused by bingo on the Tuscarora Reservation, the SNI bingo has been relatively untroubled, in part because the enterprise is run by the Nation rather than by a private individual, and because the profits are directed toward programs that benefit the people at large.

Many skilled iron and construction workers still find employment in nearby cities like Buffalo and Erie, commuting several hours each day from their homes on the reservation. Other employment opportunities are provided by the increasing number of Indian-owned businesses, some of which have developed as a result of the tax benefits available to members of the Nation, such as the tax-free sale of gasoline and cigarettes. These opportunities were first exploited by Seneca entrepreneurs such as Barry Snyder at the Seneca Hawk on Cattaraugus and Maurice John at Seneca Junction on Allegany, and then the Nation moved to take advantage of the potential profits. The Seneca Mini-Mart, at Exit 20 of the Southern Tier Expressway, opened in the summer of 1986 and sold gasoline and diesel fuel for about fifteen cents a gallon less than its non-Indian competitors, a boon to both the Nation and interstate truckers, whose rigs sometimes line the exit ramp as they wait for fuel. In the summer of 1987 the Nation purchased land near Cattaraugus for a similar enterprise in order to take advantage of traffic on roads skirting Lake Erie, including Interstate 90.

Two Indian-owned restaurants, Rossi's and Maurice's, opened in Salamanca in the 1980s, drawing their clientele from both Indian and white communities. Rossi's, next to the building originally containing Seneca Lanes and currently housing the SNI bingo operation, attracts many SNI employees as well as summer tourists seeking an alternative to the McDonald's across the street. Maurice's, in a less favorable location due to the closing of the Main Street bridge in Salamanca, was no longer open by the early 1990s. It is interesting to note that the most successful Indian businessmen on each reservation had non-Seneca wives, thereby making their children ineligible for enrollment in the Seneca Nation. It seems likely that this factor may be an incentive for economic success, since their children will be unable to inherit land or power in the Nation. It should be noted, however, that business success does not reflect a similar political philosophy, as the three leading entrepreneurs at Allegany represented three different political factions in the mid 1980s.

EDUCATION

The ability of the Nation to provide employment for so many of its members had an unforeseen side effect in that it gave an incentive for many Senecas to drop out of school because they could readily obtain semi-skilled jobs, particularly in the Recreation Department. Guidance counselors had difficulty countering this since such concerns as job advancement in the long term held little weight with teenagers who wanted immediate employment. In the mid 1970s the director of the SNI Education Department recommended to the Tribal Council that the Nation refuse full-time employment to dropouts not actively seeking a GED, but the program failed because it hindered political patronage. It was revived in the summer of 1987, and although it was strongly criticized by many parents and children regardless of educational level, this has remained policy as well as practice.

By the summer of 1986 the Seneca Nation Education Foundation was absorbed into the Education Department. The foundation was designed to last for only twenty years, and most of its funds were spent, thereby making the change logical. The absorption of the

foundation by the Education Department has resulted in politiciza-
tion of its functions, and there have been frequent changes in the
position of director. However, the Nation has successfully achieved
its aim in producing college graduates. By 1985 all of the Seneca
members of the senior class at Salamanca High School not only
graduated but also went on to college, anticipating careers in such
fields as journalism, law, psychology, engineering, computer science, and accounting. It is not clear whether the Nation will be able
to provide appropriate employment for a steady stream of college
graduates or if they will be interested in returning to Allegany.
Other involuntary resettlements have indicated that the "success"
of education programs often results in children no longer interested
in the pursuit of traditional employment (Scudder 1993, 134). Informal surveys by members of the SNI Education Department suggest
that 30 percent of those who were supported by the foundation are
currently employed by the Nation. However, this does not distinguish between those who received support for a class or two and
those who completed a bachelor's degree; it is possible that the percentage is lower in the latter category. Several factors may work to
dissuade college graduates from returning to the reservation. One is
the fact that entry-level pay scales are higher in off-reservation employment. Returnees may not be willing to start at the bottom of
the ladder, and those already in midlevel positions might resent
newer, younger employees being placed in positions of authority.
Age still has its prerogatives among the Senecas. The tradition of re-
placing administrators after each election also makes a job with the
Nation less attractive for someone seeking job security and a
chance for advancement. Another difficulty, addressed more fully
in chapter 7, is the lack of land for housing at Allegany. A returning
graduate might be unwilling to settle in a trailer on his or her parents' property.

Although the Nation is producing college graduates, a high dropout rate for those in high school continues to plague the Senecas. A
study done by the Nation (Fellows 1982, 5) indicates that Seneca
students entering first grade in the period 1964–70 dropped out of
Salamanca High School at a rate over twice that of non-Indian students. Despite the fact that less than half a point separated the IQ

scores of Indian and non-Indian students (13), only 31 percent of the Indian, as opposed to 49 percent of the non-Indian, students graduated with a Regents' diploma (6). The cohort used in this study includes children whose education began during the time of relocation as well as those who started as the communities began to enter stage three in the Scudder and Colson model, Community Formation and Economic Development. Although it is not possible to test with the data reported, it may be that there are differences between those entering school in the mid and late 1960s. Such differences, if they exist, would demonstrate the efficacy of the Nation's education programs. Female students drop out of school much more frequently than their male counterparts (8), mainly because of pregnancy. Cattaraugus County has one of the highest teen pregnancy rates in New York. There are no differences between Seneca and non-Seneca girls in this respect, although Indian girls are more likely to keep their babies while whites are more likely to give them up for adoption. The Nation decided to institute a family life class in the high school to address such topics as birth control and family responsibilities, but the school district refused. Recognizing the need, the Nation offered the course on the reservation on its own; the subsequent significant decrease in the number of teen pregnancies among Seneca girls was probably due, at least in part, to their participation in this program. Having seen its efficacy, the school district initiated discussions with the Nation on the possibility of adopting the program for use in the public schools.

The Indian Education Office in Salamanca High School has become a focal point for Seneca students, who stop by to tutor or be tutored, exchange gossip, or receive encouragement from the adult Senecas who run the program, aided by a committee of parents. Although Seneca political factionalism did intrude on the relatively smooth running of the office in the 1980s, parents and staff currently appear to be working well together. Unfortunately, few non-Indian students take advantage of the Indian culture courses, so these courses do not increase understanding between the Indian and non-Indian communities as they might. This may reflect increased tension between the two, resulting from lease negotiations and inflammatory remarks from fringe elements on each side.

TRADITIONAL AND CULTURAL ACTIVITIES

Seneca language courses, either formally within the schools or informally within the Nation, have not increased the number of Seneca speakers. Few, if any, people under the age of thirty are fluent in the language. While some elders point to this as one of the legacies of Kinzua, this would seem to be incorrect. Few children speak Seneca because few parents speak Seneca. The loss of the language should be attributed to the parental generation and the old schools; staff at both the Allegany Indian School and the Quaker School insisted that students speak only English and punished those who did not comply. It is obvious that several hours of instruction per week in the Seneca language, not reinforced in the home, is not adequate to reintroduce it, despite the best intentions of both students and teachers. The loss of the Seneca language is something regretted by young and old alike, yet few young people seem willing or able to devote the time needed to learn it, and as time goes on, there are fewer native speakers to serve as potential teachers.

The greatest repercussions from the loss of language will be felt by the Longhouse, which requires Seneca for its ceremonies. It is hard to imagine young members of a religion being preached to in a language they do not understand. How long the religion can survive in the absence of Seneca speakers is questionable, although it might be possible in the short run to bring in speakers from another Iroquois reservation. Other suggestions include turning to female speakers, using tape-recorded speeches, and adopting English.

Attendance at the Longhouse by young people has increased, yet many seem to be drawn more by the chance to demonstrate prowess in traditional dancing than by the message of Handsome Lake. Nevertheless, their heightened participation increases the chance that they will become more intimately involved. Of all the traditional activities, dance seems to have attracted the greatest number of young followers, especially among the boys, who see it as a means of gaining prestige and income as they set out on the summer pow-wow circuit. This, in turn, brings them into contact with other Indians and enhances pan-Indian identity. The fact that many of the most skilled dancers and singers are the grandchildren of past and present Longhouse leaders indicates that the role of elders in passing down cultural traditions has not been usurped by the schools, although the Seneca Youth Dancers is a popular organization among Seneca students at Salamanca High School and has stimulated interest in dance.

The summer of 1984 saw the formation of a competitive drum (a group of male singers and a large drum) aptly named the "Treaty of 1794," whose first public performance was at the Nation's first Remember the Removal Day. Although meeting with great success in its first competitions, many at Allegany did not support the drum, claiming it was not Iroquois and showed too much influence by western Indians. Others objected to the idea of competition in general. Although stung by some of the resentment, members of the drum continue to be successful at pow-wows throughout the northeast, and the group encourages the participation of new singers and dancers. Two former Indian culture teachers sing with the drum and have formed the Allegheny River Dancers, a group of young dancers (including some preschoolers) who perform at Highbanks Campground for tourists as well as for interested Indian and non-Indian organizations throughout the eastern United States.

Most obvious in the field of dance, a cultural revival is apparent in other areas as well. George Heron, president during much of the Kinzua era, has always emphasized traditional foods, growing a large garden of Indian corn, beans, and purple potatoes. Today he is the major supplier of white hominy for the traditional Iroquois corn soup. While few still make it the old way, boiling kernels with hardwood ashes until the hulls loosen and can be rinsed off, corn soup is still an important dietary staple; it is served at all the socials and fairs and is sold every Saturday by the Jimersontown Presbyterian Church. Ghost bread, plain or with beans and salt pork, is also eaten frequently; during the summer of 1986 a Seneca woman occasionally stopped by the Allegany branch of the SNI Library with fry bread sandwiches for sale, to the delight of staff and researchers alike. Interest in traditional foods by both Senecas and tourists resulted for a brief period in a Wednesday night Indian foods buffet at Rossi's Restaurant. For three decades the Jimersontown Presbyterian Church has offered a Native Foods Dinner around Thanksgiving, which draws people from a distance of more than a hundred miles and allows people like George Heron to demonstrate their skill with venison, mush, and other traditional Iroquois foods.

The increased participation of young people in pow-wows has stimulated interest in traditional dress and beadwork because costumes are required. Although the greatest interest seems to be in the fancy dance categories, which provide the most prize money and require brightly colored feathered bustles and other non-Iroquois paraphernalia, most dancers also have more traditional (i.e., nineteenth-century) costumes as well. Women are more conservative in the area of dress, needing only to add a fancy fringed shawl to the traditional costume in order to participate in women's fancy dance competition, although some devise more elaborate garb. Beadwork is done by both men and women and includes loom-made belts and armbands as well as beaded embroidery on leggings and breechclouts. Beaded earrings, necklaces, and key chains are made for sale to tourists.

While it may be true that there are fewer people who are exclusively Longhouse adherents, much of the cultural revival focuses on the Longhouse, which has become an important political and cultural symbol. Many practicing Christians attend the major ceremonials, seeing this as an important reaffirmation of their cultural heritage, and the leaders of the Longhouse are still viewed as the conscience of the communities. Many point to Longhouse opposition as the reason why women were denied suffrage for so long and why, despite years of talk, no referendum on changing enrollment from matrilineal to blood quantum (percentage of Indian "blood" or minimal number of Seneca grandparents) has ever been held. Because of this the Longhouse has been drawn into recent political controversy as each side attempted to manipulate it to support its position.

REASSESSMENT OF REMOVAL

The 1980s have been a time of reassessment, especially for younger Senecas, unaware of the political intricacies of the fight against Kinzua Dam. Unlike their parents, who remember the struggle and know firsthand both the material improvements in housing and the loss of the old closeness, many young Senecas believe their parents and grandparents did not fight hard enough against Kinzua and focus exclusively on the negative effects of the dam. This is usually accompanied by an overly romantic view of life in the old places by people who have never seen an outhouse or carried water from the river. To them, Kinzua has become a potent symbol of the loss of Seneca land, now an issue of great importance as an increased population confronts a diminished land base. More formally educated than their elders, they are aware, as Wilkinson (1987, 48) points out, that confronted with a similar situation today, the Supreme Court would probably disallow construction on the basis of a single line item in an appropriations bill, insisting instead that Congress explicitly signal its intent to break a treaty. While this does not mean that Congress would be any less willing to sever a treaty relationship, for many it stands as another indication of the injustice done to the people of Allegany. As one man poignantly stated during the 1984 Remember the Removal panel discussion, "They stopped a dam because of a tiny fish [Tellico Dam and the snail darter], but what about us? We're people; don't we count?" Even in the case of the Tellico Dam, however, the effects on the snail darter received more coverage than the effects on the Cherokees (American Indian Program 1991, 12).

The people of Allegany considered the meaning of the dam on 29 September 1984, a day proclaimed by sni president Lionel John as Remember the Removal Day "in remembrance of those Senecas who relinquished their lands, their homes, and a way of life." Because, for the most part, the day was initiated and directed by young Senecas who were children at the time of removal, this date marks the beginning of stage four, Incorporation and Handing Over, for the Seneca people individually and for the Nation, as it dealt with both the remembrance and long-term effects of relocation. The fact that influence was shifting to a new generation became more apparent as the day progressed.

Remember the Removal Day began at the old Red House Bridge over the Allegheny River on a cold, gray, rain-threatening morning. It was appropriate, President John said, that the ceremonies begin there since the old places were all located along the river. After an opening song by the Allegany Singing Society, John and former president George Heron spoke briefly, and there were emotional prayers by Ralph Bowen, pastor of the Red House Indian Chapel (now the Red House Memorial Church), and Richard Johnny-John of the Cold-spring Longhouse. A wreath tied with a black ribbon was thrown into the river as the real commemoration of removal began, a six-and-a-half-mile walk along old Route 17 from the bridge at Red House to the Steamburg community building. Several hundred marchers wearing black armbands followed a flatbed truck carrying the "Treaty of 1794" drum singing an honor song. Despite the bad weather, many elders who had been forced to relocate joined the march, but the majority of walkers were middle-aged and younger. Clearings in the trees and brush and the remains of driveways indicated the location of old homes, carefully pointed out to young children, and also showed the amount of land that, for the most part, had never been flooded. Joining the Senecas were Walt and Peggy Taylor, the former representatives of the Indian Committee of the Philadelphia Yearly Meeting of Friends, invited back by the Nation from their post in British Columbia, Arthur Lazarus, the Nation's attorney and member of the Iroquoia committee, and several other representatives of the Philadelphia Yearly Meeting. Upon the marchers' arrival at Steamburg, the ceremonies became more formal, with speeches by the local congressman and several invited guests. This was followed by a free lunch of traditional Seneca foods. On display in the community building were the survey books used to determine the compensation paid to landowners, with black-and-white photographs and descriptions of each building and parcel of land. These were of great interest to the relocatees; searching for their "old place" stimulated many recollections, as did the showing of home movies and filmed news reports made at the time. Bumper stickers and T-shirts commemorating the day were offered for sale, and the blue shirts were seen frequently around Allegany for several years.

It was during the afternoon panel discussion that the shift in emphasis to the new generation was most apparent because many of the old leaders were no longer present. This should not be construed as lack of interest since the physically and emotionally draining walk and the lengthy outdoor ceremonies would logically take their toll on the elders. The most emotional speakers tended to be younger women, whose questions centered on the loss of land, asking in particular what was to prevent them from reclaiming unflooded land below the 1,365-foot contour and pointing out the great differences between what they experienced as children in the old places and what their children and even younger siblings were experiencing in the relocation sites. Closing the day of commemoration were a dinner of traditional foods and Iroquois social dancing.

The impetus for the Remember the Removal Day was a group of Seneca women in their late twenties who formed the Seneca Women's Awareness Group (SWAG). The founders were college-educated women, some of whom had attended college in the Southwest, where they became involved in pan-Indian politics and social activism. Returning to Allegany, they decided to organize a group to discuss issues of interest to women and first held a bike safety clinic for children. Soon, however, they began to move into controversial political issues, questioning some SNI policies, especially as they related to land issues, which they saw as a traditional concern of women. Support for the group was widespread, and membership included both young and old women. Many men also looked with favor on them. Consideration of land led inevitably to a reflection on the effects of Kinzua Dam, and the idea of marking the twentieth anniversary of removal began to crystallize. They realized, however, that this was not just a woman's issue and invited men to participate in the planning, eventually submitting a proposal to the Tribal Council, which resulted in funding for the program and the proclamation of Remember the Removal Day.

In 1985 the second Remember the Removal Day was marked by a walk from the old Red House Bridge to the Haley Building in Jimersontown, where an exhibit of old pre-removal photographs was on display and a free lunch of Seneca foods was provided. Once again there was a large turnout of walkers, the majority of whom were relatively young. Several older Senecas were distressed by the fact that the commemoration included an afternoon pow-wow, the first ever held at Allegany, which they felt was inappropriate for the solemn nature of the occasion.

As it became concerned with more political questions, SWAG began to develop a more strident tone; moderate and conservative women began to withdraw as the organization became viewed as radical. In 1985 the more outspoken members became involved in the continuing saga of the Southern Tier Expressway. Adamant about the Nation incurring no additional loss of land, several of the women were among those instrumental in stopping construction on the unfinished section of Route 17 east of Salamanca. Although the Nation had signed the 1976 Agreement of Adjustment with the state of New York, it remained for the Department of Transportation to settle with individual landowners. There were no homes on the property involved, but a number of families stood to lose land, including some who had previously lost land to Kinzua Dam. The majority of the landowners reached agreement with the state, but by the summer of 1985 there were still a handful of holdouts. When the state began road construction on the property of several of these landowners, protests broke out. Joining the actual property owners were several women from SWAG and the leader of a vocal group of self-styled "traditionalists" from the Cattaraugus Reservation. The Nation refused to take an active role in the dispute, stating accurately that it was up to New York to deal with the property owners, although it was quietly working behind the scenes to end the confrontation. The Tribal Council warned that any SNI employees behind the barricades in what became known as Camp 17 would jeopardize their jobs. Two were terminated for being present after working hours, yet several leading SNI politicians organized a counterprotest against the encampment, providing release time during working hours for those willing to confront the people on the highway.

During the brief time that they held construction equipment hostage, the protesters built a small longhouse to symbolize their commitment to retaining traditional land and their hope for support from the Six Nations Confederacy at Onondaga. This support never materialized because the Confederacy refused to take a stand, determining that the issue was an internal affair of the Seneca Nation. Fighting symbol with symbol, the counterprotesters recruited one of the speakers from the Coldspring Longhouse to try to negotiate with the people at Camp 17. Although this speaker personally saw his role as that of an apolitical peacemaker, his presence was infuriating to the protesters, who saw it as a blatantly political move; perhaps they were upset too because their inability to understand his Seneca undermined their claims to be "traditionalists" in the eyes of many. An attempt to garner support during the Green Corn

Ceremony at Coldspring was rebuffed by Longhouse leaders. Betraying a deep-seated sympathy for the protesters, one elder who publicly opposed the camp said, "You know it would be different if they had a chance." Having lost the Kinzua fight, many elders were reluctant to enter into a fight that did not have a significant chance of success. Far from having been beaten down, they had opted to choose their next fight carefully.

The search for the elusive "traditional Indian" is as frustrating for Indians as it is for anthropologists. To the people at Camp 17, their claim to traditional status rested on their defense of the Seneca land base; in the words of one, "You don't have to speak Seneca to be a traditionalist." For many Senecas, anyone who both speaks Seneca and is a Longhouse member is accepted as a traditionalist, but it is clear that this is not an exclusive definition. As the protest continued, people at the encampment backed away from the "traditionalist" label, identifying themselves as "treaty Indians" or "political dissidents." Arguing against the elected government in terms reminiscent of the fight against Fisher-Price, they ignored the fact that it was under the traditional form of government by chiefs that land was lost in the Buffalo Creek Treaty and that the constitutional form of government was instituted in order to prevent further alienation of land. The strongest argument against the 1976 agreement between New York and the Nation would have been the deletion of federal approval discovered by Laurence Hauptman (1980, 100), but this was unknown to most of the protesters, as indeed it probably was to President Hoag and the Tribal Council when they supported it.

Despite the fact that there was widespread support for the reason behind the encampment, especially among older relocatees, most Senecas strongly disapproved of the methods. As one said, "They don't realize that the tradition they're claiming to uphold would not permit the tactics that they're using." Others felt that the landowners were motivated more by a desire for money than concern for land, and in fact, those who settled last did receive considerably higher payments, as was the case with those who had appealed the initial offers by the Army Corps for their land in the Kinzua take area.

The encampment also demonstrated the extent to which Kinzua Dam had become the measure of political activism for the Senecas. Camp members pointed to the dam as evidence of what they were trying to prevent. Opponents asked where the protesters were during the Kinzua era, although Kenneth Van Aernam, whose mother's property was one of the focal points of the protest, had worked against the dam with his mother, even testifying during congressional hearings (House 1964, 47–48). Other people at the encampment had not been born yet or were small children.

By fall the protests had ebbed, despite widespread national publicity, and the road was completed in the disputed area by the following summer. Several landowners whose property was taken have quietly continued their protest, refusing to accept the payment placed in an escrow account for them by the state of New York. The issues raised by SWAG and the Route 17 protest ensured that the 1986 election would be hotly contested although there were no declared candidates until the late spring.

POLITICAL PARTIES

The People's Party, in power for over a decade with only minimal opposition, had, from all reports, grown complacent, ignoring tales of wrongdoing by officials and accepting barely adequate work from some political appointees. In 1984 a reform-minded wing of the party refused to accept the party's nominee for president, instead convincing Calvin Lay, a former president and member of the People's Party, to run as an independent. Lay's election indicated that the party was in trouble. The People's Party did not even field a candidate in 1986, perhaps because its rumored choice, then SNI treasurer Lionel John, who had developed and headed the Nation's outstanding Health Department, resigned to become executive director of the United Southern and Eastern Tribes. The first announced candidate was Maurice "Moe" John, a former Hoag ally who had been arrested during the Camp 17 protest and whose newly formed party was called the Sovereign Senekas. John was well known for his willingness to do battle with New York State and the city of Salamanca over issues of taxation and application of municipal building codes to Indian-owned properties. Although he was respected by many for his courage in taking a stand on important issues, his unpredictability and penchant for overt action was seen as a potential political liability and embarrassment. The prospect of a Moe John presidency was anathema to white Salamancans.

Following rumors that he was considering reentry in the political arena, Robert Hoag announced his candidacy in early September, heading a reform coalition called the Seneca Alliance. Hoag was an equally successful businessman, so both sides seemed evenly matched in financial reserves, an important consideration since the Senecas learned vote buying early and well from white politicians. A highly skilled politician, Hoag was less radical than John, a middle-of-the-road candidate whose supporters pointed to his leadership during the halcyon days of the mid 1970s as proof that he could move the Nation out of its perceived doldrums. To a great extent this election promised to be a test of the strength of the forces of stage four of the Scudder-Colson model. Young, well-educated, and critical of many post-removal programs, both candidates wanted the Nation to emphasize its independence and "sovereignty" by reducing dependence on federal programs and strengthening ties to the Six Nations Confederacy in order to increase pan-Iroquois pressure on the state and federal governments.

An unforeseen development was the entry of Merle Watt as a third presidential candidate, heading the Seneca Coalition for Change. Watt, philosophically closer to John than Hoag, had also been at Camp 17, but the two apparently had a falling out. Although Watt was from a large and prominent family (his mother, Nettie, was the most renowned Seneca basketmaker until her death in August 1987), he could not hope to match the fund-raising efforts of his opponents. However, his entry into the race identified him as a spoiler, although it would be wrong to see Watt only as an interloper. He clearly played an important role, providing an alternative for voters suspicious of John's radicalism and Hoag's ties to the whites of Salamanca. But by splitting the more activist vote, he ensured the election of Bob Hoag as a minority president in a very close election.

Comparison of the slates of candidates for the three parties indicates significant differences. The Sovereign Senekas included more women (SWAG influence was strong), more relocatees, and younger people as candidates. The Seneca Alliance represented wealthier and older segments of the Allegany population, with fewer relocatees and fewer women. Many of the Alliance candidates either were experienced in SNI government or held white-collar jobs off the reservation; the Alliance had a clear edge in experience. The Seneca Coalition for Change slate of candidates also had a greater number of relocatees than the Alliance, but they had less experience. The party's late formation probably meant that potential candidates had already committed themselves to John or Hoag.

The transfer of power to a new generation raised primarily in the relocation sites is obviously not complete. This generation, still showing some of the trauma experienced in childhood, is better educated and more wary than the previous one. These young adults have been sensitized by removal, and their current interest in more radical politics is not merely a reflection of childhood disruption. To a great extent it represents a realistic evaluation of dam-related problems only now becoming critical. Most of the families who fought Kinzua Dam were assured of a house and a maximum of three acres. What will be available for each of the children raised in that house? That the young people have been tempered by their experiences over two decades ago is shown by their recollections. Only now are they able to express the anger and frustration and to ask the questions that have weighed heavily on many of them for so long. The problems they now confront are not imaginary; it is inevitable that there will be political repercussions as they move into power. The transition will not be easy.

SEVEN

The Legacies of Kinzua Dam

The ghosts of relocation are still apparent in the mists along the Allegheny River. In times of distress they draw relocatees back to the riverbanks for reflection and solace, a brief return to the quieter times before Kinzua Dam. It is not unusual to see a single individual or family sitting quietly along the river. It is also not unusual to see non-Indian families in recreational vehicles camped on Seneca ground, sometimes on land rented from the owners, other times simply squatting until the landowner asks them to leave. For many, the banks have a near sacred quality, and the litter of contemporary mechanized camping is seen as sacrilege. This also points to another source of tension among relocatees. Those whose land is not completely inundated are free to use it for whatever purpose they deem fit, including rental to non-Indians. This ability to continue using and profiting from land for which they received compensation rankles some whose land is totally under water. However, those with land above the water level did not receive full compensation in recognition of their retention of partial use of it.

At some point in the not-too-distant future, as the land shortage becomes more acute, it seems inevitable that some will return to land below 1,365 feet and build homes there. Several people are currently contemplating such a move. Much of the land has never been flooded, even during the floods caused by Hurricane Agnes in 1972, which devastated much of Salamanca. Although it would be impossible to get flood insurance, some might be willing to gamble that the once-in-a-century flood that would fill the pool to maximum capacity would not occur in their lifetime. This would provide only a brief respite from land pressure since land directly along the river-bank would still not be usable due to normally fluctuating reservoir levels. Utilization of the hillsides for expanded housing is an option open only to wealthier individuals able to afford construction of pri-vate access roads; it is unlikely that much building will be done in this area in the near future. More and more Senecas are choosing housing within the city of Salamanca. Indians are exempt from property taxes in the city because the land is owned by the Seneca Nation, and the removal of properties from the tax rolls as more In-dians move there has increased the tax burden on non-Indian resi-dents and serves to inflame Indian-white tension. The advantage for Senecas is that they can still participate fully in reservation life, an important consideration for many.

The shortage of land became an important issue for many youn-ger Senecas, who tended to take more outspoken positions on the Salamanca leases, which were renewed in 1991 after more than a de-cade of often acrimonious debate. The Seneca Nation Settlement Act (P.L. 101–503), signed by President George Bush on 3 November 1990, extended the leases for forty years at terms more equitable to the Seneca Nation. Compensation in the amount of $35 million for a century of unconscionable rates was made to the Nation with a per capita payment to each enrolled Seneca of $2,000. Although the uncertainty of the lease issue that had clouded Seneca-white rela-tions in the area is now removed, the bad feelings prompted by radi-cal rhetoric from extremist elements on both sides remain. The Sal-amanca Coalition of United Taxpayers (scout) continued in 1997 to fight rear guard actions that, although unsuccessful, maintained the flames of distrust. By midyear, all but one of those who refused to sign their lease had been evicted, the sole exception being an in-dividual in poor health. Allegany Senecas point out that if it were Indians who were several years behind in rental payments to white landlords, they would have been evicted long ago. The group that has particularly felt the repercussions of lease problems is Seneca schoolchildren, who have reported anti-Indian statements by teach-ers in the classroom. Unlike the Kinzua experience, young Senecas and their parents are now far better educated, familiar with the school system, and less willing to passively accept what are felt as inappropriate comments.

Education continues to be a major concern of the Nation, and in the 1992 SNI election, 77 percent of voters approved a referendum to explore the feasibility of a tribal school. Of the 1,800 students in the Salamanca City Central School District, 390 are Indian and bring the district $2 million in state aid. In February 1993, 80 pupils withdrew briefly from the district and attended a makeshift school on the reservation staffed by four certified Seneca teachers and four Seneca teacher aides. The removal of Indian children from the district would have a significant financial impact, and as the SNI continues to encourage the training and certification of teachers, it can no longer be dismissed as an idle threat.

As more enrolled Senecas leave the reservation, political problems may also increase. Because all enrolled Senecas are eligible to vote in the Nation's elections if they are present on election day, nonresident voters can be a critical factor in close races. Significant blocks of enrolled Senecas currently live in Erie and Buffalo, and it is logical to assume that their numbers will increase. Despite the fact that both cities are near enough to Allegany or Cattaraugus for significant interaction to occur, differences in perspective necessarily exist between reservation and nonreservation populations, demonstrated most clearly in land claims cases in which nonresident enrollees have tended to favor per capita distribution of the settlement whereas reservation residents want to see much of it put toward reservation development. For the Seneca Nation, increasing numbers of off-reservation enrollees may increase the chance of vote fraud if nonresidents lose interest in reservation politics and sell their votes to the highest bidder.

The initial hypothesis that women would be more severely impacted by removal than men has not been supported by this case study. While women reported slightly greater trauma, this was due more to the fact that they had to deal with the daily problems of the removal than due to gender; they also seemed more pleased with the improved housing, which definitely made household tasks easier. To a surprising extent, the benefits that came to women from the dam were greater than those for men. This is most apparent in the expansion of political and economic roles for women. Jobs created by the increasing size of the SNI government provided career choices for women not previously available, at least not on the reservation. Even though many were low-paying, low-prestige jobs, there were some avenues to advancement. As previously noted, the success of the education program was primarily due to women. Community Action Programs provided leadership and management experience for women, some of whom continued their education as adult learners, earning bachelor's and master's degrees. The right to vote and hold office, while more related to the tenor of the times than Kinzua Dam, gave women their long-sought entry into the formal political structure. The experiences of the dam fight provided them with greater insight into how Seneca, state, and federal government systems worked and probably allowed them to move more rapidly into positions of authority. It is interesting to note that many women seem to occupy instrumental roles; for example, all of the presidential candidates in the 1986 election had female campaign managers. Whether this is a holdover from the days when women's only political role was behind-the-scenes manipulation or whether it is merely coincidence is unknown. At least one politically active woman asserted to me that women's reluctance to seek the office of president was due to a distaste for the mudslinging that accompanies most campaigns but is most strongly directed toward the presidential candidates. Women have been elected to the office of treasurer, which entails heading a reservation, so there is clearly no concern on the part of the electorate or women themselves about their abilities (Bilharz and Abler 1996).

In one area, however, women have suffered disproportionately from the effects of removal. This is in the sphere of family relations, particularly those between grandmother and grandchildren. As alluded to in chapter 5, grandparents play a decreased role in their extended families, a problem that has been exacerbated because the elderly housing complex in Salamanca limits the number of overnight guests one can have and the length of their stay. This makes it impossible for grandmothers to take over the care of grandchildren whose parents are temporarily or permanently disabled through illness or substance abuse. Compilation of the list of relocatees by household demonstrated the important role played by Seneca grandmothers and other older Seneca women in caring for children who might otherwise become wards of the state. Several women in the old places were well known as "foster grandmothers." One described her role by saying, "If someone leaves a kitten on your doorstep, you take it in. How can you possibly do less for a child?" Unfortunately, today both the kitten and child would end up in a government agency if they were dropped off near the elderly complex. Still, there was at least one woman who filled this role until her death in the 1990s. Other residents of the complex have devised elaborate ruses to keep their grandchildren near, but the contact is still much less than desired by all involved. This disruption of ties between generations has also contributed to the decline in Seneca language because the grandparents' generation was the only one with a significant number of native speakers. However, it is likely that ties would have become somewhat attenuated even without removal as children increasingly preferred watching television to listening to stories by older relatives. Storytelling was declining as an art form well before Kinzua.

The impact on elders, regardless of gender, remains significant. Some cite removal as the major cause of a breakdown in extended families and the destruction of a sense of community (John 1989, 66). Of the relocated elders interviewed by Seneca sociologist Randy John, 89 percent said they preferred their "old places" without modern amenities to the relocation houses (63). This loss is felt most severely by Longhouse people (64).

As noted, children paid a particularly high price during removal because they lacked an effective means of dealing with their grief. During a 1985 conference organized by the Seneca Women's Awareness Group, participants, most of whom were children at the time of removal, were unable to identify a single good thing that happened between 1965 and 1970, an indication of the depth and extent of the trauma. It needs to be emphasized, however, that not all children reported severe reactions. Those whose parents were more directly involved, and who were therefore more knowledgeable about the removal, seem to have coped best with relocation both then and now. Those who were children at the time do express more anger, but this anger may be less reflective of trauma than the contemporary confrontation of the long-term effects of the dam. Better educated than their parents, many are intellectually aware of the historical chronology of events leading up to Kinzua but sadly deficient in understanding what their parents went through, due in part to parental refusal or inability to discuss the ordeal with them. A similar unwillingness to discuss traumatic events, particularly among themselves, is shown by the Mohawks of Akwesasne confronting the fallout from their 1990 "civil war" over gaming (Bilharz 1996). Combining the political skills observed in their parents with improved education, the people now moving into power will be worthy opponents for outsiders seeking to manipulate them.

The institutionalized bureaucracy is probably the most obvious legacy of the dam to the Nation. Jobs have increased, but so has political patronage and its inherent evils. As presaged by the industrial development problems of the early 1970s (the failure of the U.S. Pillow Corporation, the loss of a Fisher-Price plant, the unsuccessful Iroquoia recreational area), the 1848 system of two-year terms for the SNI executive branch, while adequate for the nineteenth century, seriously reduces the effectiveness of the president, regardless of political party or philosophy. As currently practiced, the winning party tends to spend its first year in office rewarding friends and punishing opponents and its second year preparing for the upcoming election. Expanding the executive terms to four years would permit a continuation of the spoils system (which is too well established to disappear completely) but would also provide a two-year interim during which significant achievements could occur. The staggered terms of councilors can now provide a necessary brake on an executive with delusions of grandeur. The major accomplishments of the Hoag administrations in the mid 1970s were possible because of the total domination of the People's Party; they occurred despite the system rather than because of it. Even though many elections have been dominated by a single party, internal factions made it impossible to repeat the unity that occurred in the Hoag era.

Some changes in government structure have been necessitated by the increasing number and complexity of issues facing the Seneca Nation. On 30 December 1993 President Barry Snyder relinquished his duties as chief administrative officer in order to devote more time to policy development. A new position of executive ad-

ministrative director, reporting directly to the executive, was created to oversee ongoing government programs. This change came at
a time when the Senecas were facing two issues critical to their Nation's future: economic development and taxation.

Reduction in federal aid and the uncertainty of the tax issue has
led to a greater concern with economic issues, in particular the creation of jobs since unemployment in the Nation is high. The huge
success of gaming as a source of jobs and income for the Oneidas in
both New York and Wisconsin has led many to focus on casino
(class III) gaming as a long-term route to financial stability and independence. In a nonbinding referendum held on 10 May 1994, the
Senecas voted 650–203 against casinos on the reservations, 496–
367 against Indian-owned casino gambling at a nonreservation location, and 714–446 against any class III gaming. Emotions ran
high, with isolated outbreaks of violence culminating in a shootout
on the Cattaraugus Reservation in 1995 that left three men dead.
Subsequent investigation indicated that one of the fatal bullets was
fired by the victim's son. People were horrified by the extent of division within the Nation and its tragic outcome, and the situation
remained tense as they struggled to find ways to begin a healing
process.

The 1996 election was widely viewed as a contest between pro-
and anti-gaming factions. Although the media and many other
groups predicted that Seneca businessman Ross John would win in
a landslide, even to the extent that Buffalo businesses were rumored
to be discussing casinos with him, the surprise winner was Michael
Schindler, a soft-spoken former ironworker and political neophyte
who stressed issues of sovereignty and who was opposed to hitching
the Nation's future to the lure of casinos. Given the previous strong
vote against gaming, it is hard to understand why the media assumed a victory by Ross John. Although John and Schindler have
different ideas about future development, there is strong agreement
that the Nation cannot endure another year like 1995.

The second issue is the long-simmering dispute with New York
State over the issue of taxation. A federal Supreme Court decision
to let stand a lower court decision (*Department of Taxation and Finance v. Milhelm Attea and Bros., Inc.*) permitting the state to tax
those supplying gas to Seneca retailers resulted in ongoing negotia-

tions between the sni, other Iroquois nations, and New York. Governor George Pataki, elected in November 1994, stated his intent to end tax-free sales to non-Indians. On 1 April 1997 all shipments of gasoline, diesel fuel, and cigarettes to the Seneca Nation were cut off. Unlike all the New York Iroquois except the Akwesasne Mohawks, the Seneca Nation refused to sign an interim agreement not to sell gas and cigarettes. As supplies dwindled, hundreds of Seneca and non-Seneca workers were laid off. Receiving strong support from non-Indians, who were motivated in part by the desire to continue to buy cheap gas and cigarettes but also by guilt over previous wrongs, the Seneca Nation vowed to stand firm on what it defined as a critical issue of Seneca sovereignty. Local merchants not in competition with Indian markets prominently displayed signs supporting the Seneca stance. The governor and his allies, owners of local grocery stores and gas stations, were confronted with strongly worded editorials and letters to the editor supporting the Senecas. To many, the specter of a governor who claimed a large budgetary surplus and promised to cut taxes "picking on the underdog" was an embarrassment, and signs and T-shirts proclaiming him "George Custer Pat*ax*i—Indian Hater" were common at all demonstrations. Indian supporters pointed to tax breaks given to non-Indian businesses and saw the state's position as hypocritical; if taxes were the problem, then the governor could best address the problem by lowering them for everyone so that the economic advantage the Indians had would be eliminated. These feelings increased when trucks carrying propane for heating houses were confiscated by New York State Police and when Senecas began to run out of heating fuel as the temperatures dipped into the high teens. Rosalyn Hoag, the widow of Robert Hoag and the mayor of the city of Salamanca, sent a strongly worded letter to the governor noting that the city and its residents depended on the Seneca Nation for fire and ambulance service, which was imperiled by the embargo.

On Sunday, 13 April 1997, a quickly organized show of support by whites in the city of Buffalo ended in a motorcade to the Cattaraugus Reservation and a rally with Senecas. Walking along Route 438 through the reservation, protestors climbed down an embankment and onto the New York State Thruway (Interstate 90). Carrying U.S. flags and purple and white Hau-de-nau-sau-nee banners depicting the Confederacy or Hiawatha wampum belt, they brought traffic to a halt. Although some shoving and heated exchanges occurred, the protest in general was peaceful.

A larger rally was held the following Sunday, drawing over a thousand Senecas and their Indian and non-Indian supporters. Traffic was stopped for nearly twenty-four hours on the three major roads running from Erie to Buffalo through the Cattaraugus Reservation and on Route 17 through the Allegany Reservation. The outnumbered New York State Police, in full riot gear, were forced to retreat as the Cattaraugus demonstration turned violent. The head of the state police in western New York was forced to the ground and suffered a separated shoulder, another officer was sprayed with pepper spray, and numerous Indians were clubbed. Police reinforcements arriving Sunday night from across the state effectively isolated the Cattaraugus Reservation through much of the next day, with no one allowed to enter or leave, and violence again erupted, resulting in the beating and arrest of a Cattaraugus councilor. By nightfall, representatives of the governor had arrived at the airport in Dunkirk, New York, hoping to meet with Seneca president Michael Schindler. Throughout the weeks after the embargo, Schindler kept a low profile, urging restraint on both sides and expressing sympathy for all who were injured, but at the same time he never wavered from his refusal to deal on the taxation issue. The standoff between the Seneca Nation and New York State created a common focus for feuding factions within the Nation, now united in a way unimaginable the previous year.

The major roads closed by the protesters and the police have their origins in Kinzua Dam. The Seneca Nation agreed to sell an easement through the Cattaraugus Reservation to New York for the state Thruway in order to get money to fight against dam construction. The old two-lane Route 17 through the Allegany Reservation was replaced by a limited access four-lane highway due to condemnation resulting from the construction of the dam. Land for both roads was taken as an easement so that if the roads are no longer needed, title reverts to the Seneca Nation.

Indeed, this may have contributed to the conclusion of the crisis. On 12 May the Seneca Nation requested New York to provide documentation of the right-of-way agreements for Routes 5, 20, 438, 17 (the Southern Tier Expressway), and Interstate 90 (the Thruway) within ten days. A similar request was made for rights-of-way for utilities crossing Nation land. At the same time the Tribal Council accused New York of violation of the federal Indian Gaming Regulatory Act by locating lottery machines in the city of Salamanca. Citing the absence of a gaming compact between the Nation and New York as well as the results of the 1994 referendum, the Senecas requested the U.S. attorney's office to have the machines removed.

Three days later New York Supreme Court judge Rose H. Sconiers directed the State of New York to remove the police blockade of the Seneca reservations. On 16 May State Appellate Division justice Samuel Green agreed with Sconiers's opinion that the state could not interfere with fuel or tobacco deliveries to the Nation. Within twenty-four hours trucks carrying fuel were back on the reservations. As expected, New York appealed. However, on 22 May, exactly ten days after the Seneca request, Governor Pataki, in Buffalo, announced that he had ordered the repeal of state regulations mandating the collection of state taxes on reservation sales of fuel and cigarettes to non-Indians and promised to send to the legislature a bill amending the state tax law. The next day the front page headline of the *Buffalo News* announced, "Indians win tax war." Although there were deep divisions among other Iroquois groups as to how to respond to the tax crisis, ironically, at the end, it was the Seneca Nation, long considered the most conservative of the Iroquois, that stood united and alone against New York.

By July the governor and legislature were embroiled in a battle over the latest budget in New York history, and with peace restored to highways and reservations, the tax issue had receded in importance. Lobbyists for convenience store operators and petroleum marketers were furious with the governor and announced they would fight his proposed legislation. At the end of the month the Appellate Court overturned Sconiers's ruling. Both New York and the Seneca Nation will hold elections in 1998, and the ultimate disposition of the tax issue is likely to become a political issue in the campaigns.

Despite high unemployment among Senecas, the relative abundance of jobs seems to have negatively impacted the spirit of volunteerism so apparent during the Kinzua era. Programs that provided even token remuneration established a precedent of payment for activities previously undertaken for free. A universal complaint among Allegany Senecas is that everything is political, an accurate assessment since the system almost demands it. Even Robert Hoag at the height of his power was not immune. In 1978 he was indicted on charges of vote fraud and misappropriation of funds. The government's case rested almost entirely on the testimony of an admitted substance abuser (later recovered), and Hoag was eventually acquitted on all counts. There are obvious parallels with the cases of the chairs of the Standing Rock and Cheyenne River Reservations noted in chapter 3.

The Nation is also studying the future course of law enforcement on the reservation. Until recently, white district justices heard charges against Indians and often seemed to ignore the rights of Indian victims, particularly if the perpetrator was also Indian. A good example of this occurred in the mid 1980s when a Seneca patrolman was assaulted by another Seneca when he answered a domestic disturbance call. As a result of the attack he was hospitalized overnight with head injuries. It took nearly a week for a warrant to be issued for the assailant, who was eventually placed on probation. Several weeks later an off-duty white law officer was "slapped" by a white man. In this case, in which, according to news reports, no injuries resulted, the assailant received six months in jail and five years probation. "Trouble on the reservation" has not been a high priority for the Cattaraugus County Sheriff's Department, although steps have been taken to improve relations between the Nation and local law enforcement agencies. In the time immediately following removal, a representative of the sheriff's department was at the Haley Building once a week to answer questions and encourage good relations. Once this program stopped, the situation seems to have deteriorated. The fault does not lie entirely with the sheriff's department. Talk about sovereignty and independence makes it difficult for non-Indian law enforcement agencies to know just what is acceptable intervention. A solution to this was worked out in December 1993 when SNI police officers were sworn in as Cattaraugus County sheriff's deputies, thus permitting them to make arrests on Seneca land; this agreement was not renewed by the Senecas in 1996.

The increased visibility of the Seneca Nation in the broader community was apparent by the mid 1970s. Since that time Indians have been elected to the school board, have served as head of the Selective Service Board, have been elected Homecoming King and Queen at Salamanca High School, and have served as president of the high school senior class. In addition, Senecas have been moving into important positions in government and pan-Indian affairs. George Abrams sat on the board of trustees of the Museum of the American Indian–Heye Foundation, Dr. Hazel Dean-John headed the Native American Unit of the New York State Department of Education, Lionel John was executive director of the United Southern and Eastern Tribes, and a number of Senecas have served in important positions with the BIA in Washington. The recreational facilities of the Haley Building are used by white groups from Salamanca, thereby increasing interaction between the two groups. The Nation's gas station and convenience store also provided a new site for regular interaction, which might result in improved lines of communication and friendship. Unfortunately, the high levels of animosity generated by the prolonged lease negotiations and the presence of a branch of the Ku Klux Klan in Salamanca may work against forces for unity in the short run.

Conclusion

The preceding chapters may lead one to conclude that the long-term effects of relocation can frequently be beneficial, especially if enough advisers and monies are provided for the relocatees. This, however, would be erroneous. While some individuals and communities survive, others do not. To fully appreciate the success of the Senecas it is useful to compare their experiences with those of other Indian groups whose relocation occurred within five years of the Seneca removal. That the two examples chosen are from native groups in Canada does not signify differences between the U.S. and Canadian approaches; indeed, they are remarkably similar.

COMPARISONS WITH CONTEMPORARY RELOCATIONS

The reality of failed relocation was made explicit on 23 January 1993 when six Innu (Naskapi) children from Davis Inlet on the northern coast of Labrador were discovered by a native police officer sniffing gasoline in an unheated shed in temperatures of forty below zero (Celsius) and screaming that they wanted to die. Videotapes of the children were shown on television stations throughout the world. The decision to make the tape available was made by Peter Penashue and George Rich, Innu Nation president and vice president respectively, in order to draw attention to problems facing the community of five hundred Innus. The immediate result was that the Canadian government doubled its funding to the band to $8,365,085 (U.S.$6,535,223), or $16,730 per capita (U.S.$13,070), and plane loads of would-be helpers representing private and public agencies descended on Davis Inlet.

A year later Davis Inlet could point to extensive repairs on existing houses, six new houses, a youth recreation center, a chlorinated water supply, a successful job-training program, and more trained Innu community development workers and alcohol counselors. Band council chief Katie Rich noted that only half of the adults are chronic problem drinkers or alcoholics, down from 73 percent in 1993 (Valpy 1994, D5). Of the eighteen children sent to Poundmakers, an Alberta addiction treatment center for native people, thirteen are reported to continue abusing solvents. On New Year's Eve 1994, six of them trashed a safe house for victims of domestic and sexual violence, the Royal Canadian Mounted Police (RCMP) patrol cabin, a school, and a new restaurant. Chief Rich requested that the RCMP remove them from the community. While some tangible improvement can be seen at Davis Inlet, it is equally obvious that it remains a grossly dysfunctional community. One federal official noted, "What's missing from Davis Inlet is the sense of hope." Another confirmed this by saying, "There are lots of shitty communities where the heart still beats strong, but not in Davis Inlet" (quoted in Valpy 1994, D1).

The Innus were relocated to Davis Inlet in 1967 after the priest and a government official persuaded them to move from a tent village to a place where they were promised houses, furnaces, clean water, sanitation, and a school for their children. When they arrived at the island location, they discovered that many houses did have toilets and bathtubs but that there was no running water; in fact, the houses had no pipes. Water was obtained from a central pump, but buckets were used as toilets. A communal laundry and shower was closed because the septic system did not work; the building is currently used as a storeroom. The houses for the white teachers and the Catholic mission have both running water and a septic system (Gray 1997a).

Patterns of leadership adapted to bush living were not easily transferred to more permanent habitations, and a culture based on sharing was replaced by a cash economy. The relocation site was chosen because the deep harbor provided a good site for a government wharf. The social and cultural implications of restriction to an island for three or four months each year were apparently not considered. Many Innus turned to alcohol. On Valentine's Day 1992, six children died in a house fire when the adults were out drinking. There was no water to put out the blaze. The horror of the children's deaths led to a collective soul-searching within the community, and there was talk of moving to a new location. Although most Innus stopped drinking for a while, drinking to excess began again when no progress was made toward relocation. Following the children's suicide attempts, the Davis Inlet Innus again began to talk about relocating (DeMont 1994; Gray 1997a).

In December 1996 the Canadian government agreed to spend $85 million (U.S.$63 million) to move the 550 Innus to a new location, which they themselves have chosen, on Sango Bay, fifteen kilometers (nine miles) to the west. Here they have been promised houses with appropriate amenities. Many Innus saw this as a chance for a new start that will be carefully planned and that will avoid previous mistakes. Reflecting this outlook, the Innu committee in charge of the move is called Renewal. Initial optimism, however, has begun to fade as people realize that the move will not take place for another five to eight years; again there has been an increase in alcohol abuse, although now only about 60 percent of the adults are considered problem drinkers (Gray 1997a).

The attention focused on Davis Inlet might suggest a uniquely aberrant situation, yet a comparison with the Ojibwas of Grassy Narrows, Ontario, indicates that the disintegration of an entire community may not be all that unusual. Many abortive resettlements probably escape public or academic attention because of their brief duration or the small population involved.

Kai Erickson, whose 1978 study of the Buffalo Creek, West Virginia, flood dealt with both individual and collective trauma, described the people of Grassy Narrows as "more deeply damaged than any community I had ever seen. Or heard about. Or even imagined" (quoted in Shkilnyk 1985, xiii). The odds that someone from this reserve will die from violence are three in four, although prior to relocation 91 percent of the deaths were from natural causes (9, 11). In just one year over a third of the children aged five through fourteen were removed from their homes because of abuse, neglect, or abandonment (10). In a population that numbered 490 in 1977, 26 children between the ages of eleven and nineteen (17 percent of this age cohort) attempted suicide; this is probably an undercount as it includes only those attempts in which police were involved (16–17). During the same school year, only 5 of the 69 children between the ages of fifteen and nineteen were in high school at the beginning of the second quarter. Across all grades the dropout rate was 46 percent (34–35). Nearly a third of children aged eight through fifteen were on probation for criminal activity (30). Substance abuse in the form of alcohol and gas sniffing was rampant. Anastasia Shkilnyk (44) found children as young as three engaged in gas sniffing, with the result that permanent brain damage was apparent by the time the children entered first grade. As with the Innus of Davis Inlet (Valpy 1994, D1) observers at Grassy Narrows noted that listlessness, passivity, and indifference were far greater than that encountered in Third World countries (Shkilnyk 1985, 4). "In the span of only one generation after the relocation of Grassy Narrows, the central institutions of the Ojibwa culture, the people's moral values and beliefs, customary relationships, political organization, and mode of production—all were rendered impotent, useless, even superflous [sic] under the imposed conditions of the new reserve" (175).

The relocation of the Grassy Narrows Ojibwas occurred in 1963 when the government decided it would be easier to provide them with services at a new settlement five miles south of their village (Shkilnyk 1985, 2). It is clear that the government was mostly concerned with its own convenience. As with the Davis Inlet Innus, and unlike the case of the Allegany Senecas, the stated intention of this relocation was to benefit primarily, if not exclusively, the relocatees themselves. Logically, therefore, one might expect the results of the move to be positive, as these were not peoples "in the way" of a large national or regional development program. Both groups numbered approximately five hundred and were promised an improved standard of living.

The experience of the Allegany Senecas stands in stark contrast to the Grassy Narrows Ojibwas, but it is important to note the similarities as well as to account for the differences. For both, extended family ties were important and formal political institutions were weak or nonexistent prior to relocation (Shkilnyk 1985, 79). After removal there was a shift in leadership to younger men with greater experience in the non-Indian world, although the dominance of the People's Party among the Senecas contrasts sharply with the rapid turnover in leadership experienced by the Ojibwas, who had eleven chiefs between 1963 and 1977 (102, 104). Changes in settlement patterns were apparent, as were changes in the nature and function of government, as both groups saw increased amounts of federal and state or provincial aid flow into their reserves (123). Anti-Indian discrimination continued in nearby white communities even though the latter were dependent upon Indian monies for their survival (125, 130). Influenced by the rise of the American Indian Movement, young Indians adopted more confrontational methods in response, which was of concern to their elders (132). Many had a new interest in understanding why relocation occurred and felt anger when it was realized that removal was largely a by-product of technical and engineering concerns (170).

Older Indians in both groups complained about the proximity of houses and resultant problems of wandering children and dogs. The decline in family gardens was also mourned and blamed on poor soil conditions (Shkilnyk 1985, 139). In each group those who chose not to settle in the new areas were on their own when it came to housing (172). Although both groups noted improvements in housing, these were far greater for the Senecas, whose houses all had indoor plumbing, whereas at Grassy Narrows twenty years after removal only a handful of houses had water or sewage hookups (173). Some continued to return to their old homes. Formerly living along beautiful river banks, they were now relegated to mud flats (Allegany) and a stagnant lake (Grassy Narrows) (173–74).

In accounting for the differences between the groups, one should note that the people of Grassy Narrows were not suffering solely from the effects of an involuntary removal. In 1970 high levels of methyl mercury were found in the waters of the English-Wabigoon river system. Not only had the river been a source of subsistence for many Ojibwas, but it had also provided cash and jobs from commercial fishing and guiding at tourist camps, all of which were now impossible. Apart from the economic impact, the people of Grassy

Narrows had to cope with the realization that the river that had been an important focal point of their lives was a source of danger— past, present, and future. Although few showed dangerous levels of mercury in their bodies (193, 197), there was great concern with what might happen in the future, especially because of sensational- ist stories in the press comparing Grassy Narrows with the Min- amata mercury disaster in Japan (214–15). This chronic fear and insecurity about health and safety was not felt by the Senecas, al- though a few individuals continued to express concern over possi- ble political termination.

WHY ALLEGANY IS DIFFERENT

The differences between Allegany and Grassy Narrows, however, cannot all be attributed to environmental pollution at the latter. The paths each community would take were strongly divergent be- fore the mercury was discovered.

Twenty years after removal, the Allegany Senecas were a vibrant community with a strong sense of identity and a range of problems not unlike those confronting the surrounding non-Indian areas. Davis Inlet and Grassy Narrows, on the other hand, were caught in a downward spiral of despair and disintegration to the extent that the term *community* almost seems inappropriate. What can ac- count for such an extreme contrast?

One difference is the degree of geographic isolation of each group. Although Grassy Narrows, Davis Inlet, and Allegany were all rural communities, Allegany was notably closer to large population cen- ters than the Canadian communities, and the Senecas had a history of farming and of dependence on wage labor, especially among males, extending back for at least a century. The impact of removal on subsistence was therefore much less, despite the fact that hunt- ing and collecting were significantly reduced.

Group size and subsistence patterns are other obvious dissimi- larities. There were about 20 percent more Allegany Senecas relo- cated (if those who lost land in addition to houses are included) as inhabitants of Grassy Narrows or Davis Inlet. Because not all res- idents were involved in self-destructive behaviors, the core of healthy individuals would have been larger at Allegany. Even dur-

ing the worst times of anger and demoralization, there was no indication of anything approaching the level of substance abuse found
in the Canadian reserves. Widespread alcohol abuse occurred at
Grassy Narrows only after relocation and is clearly a result of it
(Shkilnyk 1985, 11). In fact, the only clear parallels between conditions at Davis Inlet and Grassy Narrows are with the Senecas at the
end of the eighteenth century on the eve of the Handsome Lake revitalization movement.

The most critical variables lie within the cultural realm. While
the Senecas and the Ojibwas both valued individual independence,
and contributions of both men and women to group survival were important, the traditional sedentary villages of the Senecas, centered
around matrilineages, provided a more stable focus for community
development and a more formal government structure. Traditional
Iroquois sociopolitical organization in the form of the Confederacy
Condolence Ceremony and moiety organization provided a framework whereby some of the strain of relocation could briefly be
borne by the opposite group. In this way the unusual governmental
structure of the Seneca Nation provided a distinct advantage in that
council members from Cattaraugus shared the responsibilities of
administration and also served the traditional condoling functions
of wiping the tears, opening the throats, and clearing the minds of
the Allegany people grieving for their lost homes.

That the residents of Allegany could turn to people other than
outsiders was important. Unlike many groups confronting disaster,
they *knew* that their world survived and continued; there would be
Senecas there to help, called by centuries of Iroquois tradition. Also
called, albeit by a somewhat shorter tradition, were the Quakers of
the Philadelphia Yearly Meeting. The century and a half of Quaker
experience with the Seneca settlements along the Allegheny River,
while not without occasional resentment and misunderstanding,
had resulted in feelings of mutual respect and trust. Unlike the del-
uge of outsiders who descended upon Davis Inlet and remained only
briefly, the Quakers sent a single family who settled into the community and made it clear that they would remain for as long as they
could help and were wanted. Where the Cattaraugus Senecas provided important moral and cultural support, the Quakers provided
political acumen and public relations expertise, initially lacking at

both Cattaraugus and Allegany. The emergence of new leaders such as George Heron and their acquisition of these skills ensured that the Senecas did not become dependent on outsiders. Furthermore, the Quakers did nothing to encourage dependence. This combination of factors meant that the Senecas could mount an active resistance to removal. Although this resistance failed to reach its goal, it reemerged to take the dominant role in planning the new communities and setting the course for the Seneca Nation. Rather than the indifference, listlessness, and passivity found at Grassy Narrows and the absence of hope at Davis Inlet, Jimersontown and Steamburg evolved as true communities that would never forget the past but were firmly focused on the future.

The success of the Allegany Senecas cannot be attributed solely to the contributions of formal sociopolitical structures of either indigenous or foreign origin. The tremendous impact of Seneca women was critical. Many of the most acute problems facing Grassy Narrows and Davis Inlet are found among children, the products of a near total breakdown in parenting. Shkilnyk (1985, 158–60) notes that at Grassy Narrows women have borne the brunt of relocation. With traditional subsistence patterns destroyed and wage employment not an option, women's contributions were no longer necessary for survival; three-quarters of them became very heavy drinkers, resulting in the abuse, neglect, or abandonment of their children.

Among the Senecas, women have never ceased to be the focus of family organization. The impact of Euro-American society, especially in the post-Revolutionary period, was much less on females than males, and even the social gospel of Handsome Lake recognized the importance of women despite its new emphasis on patrilineal nuclear families. Matrilineal descent meant that women never doubted their importance socially or culturally. The centrality of this knowledge in women's lives cannot be underestimated. They remained, in the minds of men and women alike, the "mothers of the nation." Despite denial of formal political participation from 1848 to 1964, Seneca women retained a vital interest in their society, utilizing whatever forums were available (e.g., volunteer work, committee assignments) to maintain their traditional roles even in vastly changed circumstances. In the times surrounding removal, Seneca women not only were instrumental in setting policies in housing and education but also continued their central role within the home. Their increased involvement in outside activities reduced the amount of time they were able to spend with their children, and in many cases they found themselves unable or unwilling to share their grief and fears. Although the women believed this would alleviate some of the pressure felt by the children, ironically it served to increase their stress by denying them both information and an interpretive framework. Despite this, children saw their mothers (and fathers) as active, often angry, participants rather than as passive, withdrawn victims. Families did not disintegrate. While some relocatees reported an increase in alcohol consumption among men, at no time did it result in any long-term disability, except in those whose alcohol problems long predated Kinzua. No one reported widespread serious substance abuse among women. By maintaining and building upon traditional Iroquois gender roles, they provided good models for their children, both male and female, so that a pattern of dysfunctional families was not established. The attitudes and actions of women illustrate the starkest contrast between Allegany and Grassy Narrows and go a long way in explaining the differences between the two reserves.

EVALUATING THE SCUDDER-COLSON MODEL

The primary intent of this case study was to document the long-term impact of forced relocation on the people of the Allegany Reservation and the Seneca Nation and to test the utility of the model proposed by Thayer Scudder and Elizabeth Colson. The Allegany Senecas differ from many of the groups used in the initial formulation of the model, which was developed in the context of rural Third World populations. Although an ethnic minority, the Senecas were literate, spoke English, and had a formal government at the time of relocation. The unique structure of their government, reflecting geographically separate reservations and composed of equal numbers of elected representatives from both, meant that government decisions about the removal were made by a body only half of whose members were actual or potential relocatees. The other half were therefore able to deliberate in a less emotional atmosphere. It might be argued that this process diluted the concerns of those most involved; there have been instances in which residents of each reservation have made disparaging comments about the relative losses and contributions of the other. Overall, however, the Seneca government and traditional Iroquois values proved particularly appropriate for this, and perhaps any other, disaster.

Overall, the four-stage model (Scudder and Colson 1982; Scudder 1997) is valuable in describing the Allegany relocation. Scudder's revision (1993), which separates the first stage into Planning and Initial Development and generates a five-stage model, does not fit the data as well. Scudder himself (1993, 130) has voiced some reservations about this distinction. Suggestions for a dam on the upper Allegheny had been made for nearly half a century but did not reach the planning stage until a particular constellation of political events fell into place. Whether this period and the brief time between the legal clearance for the construction of Kinzua Dam and the removal itself can be usefully separated is doubtful. Certainly investment in some areas was curtailed because of the possibility of a dam. This is seen most clearly in the refusal by the Rural Electrification Agency to extend power lines to the Cornplanter Grant across the state line in Pennsylvania in the 1940s (Deardorff 1941, 13). The fact that Allegany had formal reservation status, unlike the Cornplanter Grant, may have insulated it from some early impacts.

Effective aid to relocatees in the first two stages must be residence-based, long-term, advisory only, and disinterested. Unlike some environmental groups that may tie themselves to an indigenous anti-resettlement cause in order to further their own agenda, the Quakers were motivated by their long-standing commitment to the Senecas. At a time when previous relations based on trust have been disrupted or destroyed, only those individuals or groups that are well known to most members of the community and have earned their respect and affection have a chance of providing useful aid. This requires residence within the community, not on its periphery as in Davis Inlet, and a long-term commitment. Short-term stays only enhance distrust and suspicion. It is critical that these individuals function solely as advisers and recognize that the people have the right not to follow that advice. This has two positive functions: it enhances the relocatees' feelings of being in control and greatly decreases the chances of the adviser becoming a scapegoat

for failed projects. Finally, it is obvious that government bureaucrats, regardless of how well intentioned they are, will be less effective than people perceived as disinterested. For the Senecas, the
long history of Quaker involvement in times of tribulation made
the Taylors' entry into the community relatively easy. Sid Carney,
even though he was Indian and lived in the community, was a BIA
official, which placed some limits on his effectiveness. A last point
in this regard is that advisers should not outstay their welcome.
Taylor left shortly after the last family was removed, although he
kept in close contact with friends on the reservation. Carney, assigned by the BIA and with less control over his actions, remained
longer and inevitably became involved in Seneca politics. The logical time at which advisers should leave is toward the end of the second stage, Adjustment and Coping, though recognizing this at the
time may be difficult.

The stress described by Scudder and Colson as typical of the second stage is apparent among the Senecas; however, the model in
this case is least applicable for this period. In part this reflects its
level of generality as noted by Chris de Wet (1993, 322), although he
sees this as most problematic in the final stages. William Partridge
(1989, 382) also notes that the model is somewhat inconsistent in
that the conservative response resulting from multidimensional
stress gives way to adaptation, which suggests that there was at
least some innovation and exploratory behavior during the period
of cultural involution. Scudder's (1997) refinement of the model, in
which he changes the name of the second stage from Transition to
Adjustment and Coping, takes note of this criticism. The nature of
the Seneca government makes it possible to separate the stress
from the initial planning for relocation because the people involved
were not the same, even though there was a significant overlap. The
inconsistency noted by Partridge is therefore not found in the Allegany Senecas, and this case study indicates that cultural conservatism and innovation can occur simultaneously. However, this example is probably exceptional and due to factors not readily found
elsewhere. Nevertheless, more attention needs to be paid to potential differences between political responses made by indigenous
governments or organizations and the sociocultural responses
made by relocatees on an individual as well as community basis.

This second stage is problematic in part because it does not deal with the differential effects of removal across generations. The model suggests that the handing over of power and authority that marks the final stage involves a generation born and raised in the relocation communities, but this may not be the case. For the Senecas, the torch was passed to members of a generation born in the "old places" and old enough to recall the toll that relocation took on themselves and their parents. Understanding the processes leading to and from the final stage requires knowledge of what happened to children during stage two and how they subsequently interpreted and reinterpreted those events. Colson suggests (in Scudder 1993, 132) that children can cope if they are not separated from the people to whom they look for protection. Parents and children remained emotionally and physically close during the Kinzua era, but that did not protect the children from great trauma. Seeing but not understanding what was happening increased their anxiety; parental attempts to protect them from stress served only to increase it. The failure to provide an appropriate mechanism for children to deal with their emotional reactions in part laid the groundwork for their later political activism as adults and explains its strong emotional content. Other researchers (Oliver-Smith 1991, 133; Scudder 1993, 139) have noted that resettlement provides a fertile context for the rise of political activism but have not examined the role young people play in its development. The Seneca Nation's incorporation of children's desires for the future, especially in the field of education, is probably unique in resettlement planning and was certainly beneficial. However, it emphasized the material aspect of resettlement without touching the underlying emotional pain. Ironically, this reflects the perspective of most of the individuals who plan relocations.

Scudder (1997, 682) states that the third stage begins with the naming of physical features and an increased emphasis on community rather than family developments, as demonstrated by the growth of social welfare institutions. The various clubs and organizations that sprang up at Allegany are, I believe, indicative of a conservative response more typical of stage two. Since kinship played only a small role in the selection of relocation communities, these groups, while not diminishing kin ties, served to emphasize Seneca and community identity by integrating people in age-graded organizations. They also provided a social framework within which people could shape their expectations for the future. Discussions with people who belonged to these different clubs, especially those between the ages of twenty-five and fifty, suggests that they were primarily future-oriented and that although people spoke of their sadness and anger, the focus was on social solidarity and support as well as visions of the future. These were new organizations that formed as a result of relocation. Their demise signaled that people were beginning to feel at home and that stage three, Community Formation and Economic Development, had been attained. As noted by Norman Uphoff (1991, 498), the most successful organizations were those that concentrated on only a few activities. Following the rise and fall of these organizations provides a useful measure of the passage from stage two to three. By the end of stage three, those organizations that continued to meet community needs and desires became institutionalized as departments within the Seneca Nation government.

Increased attention should be paid to the roles of voluntary organizations and participation in them by less powerful segments of the population. The Seneca experience strongly suggests that their roles may be equal to or surpass those of some of the more formal organizations and that they may open the route to power for previously disenfranchised groups. These organizations provide an important training ground for future leaders as well as the initial framework for expanded social, political, and economic activities. Finally, they provide an outlet for frustration and stress that allows individuals to see themselves as actors rather than victims.

Evidence of increased alcohol use during the second stage should be weighed against the possibility of an increased awareness of the problem. Most observers agreed that while use increased during the time immediately surrounding removal, it decreased as people began to adapt to the new communities. There is no doubt that substance abuse was and is a problem at Allegany, as it is in many communities, but it has never approached the levels recorded at Grassy Narrows and Davis Inlet. The Nation has moved boldly, if not always effectively, to deal with this problem, often doing so before surrounding white communities.

The increased emphasis on education that the model predicts as indicative of the third stage, Community Formation and Economic Development, occurred much earlier with the Senecas. Before removal was completed, they had already decided on the central position of education and had determined to use a significant portion of the rehabilitation funds to ensure postsecondary education. That the model does not account for this difference reflects its bias toward rural relocations in Third World countries. In stable capitalist or socialist societies an emphasis on increased educational opportunities may arise early in the second stage or even in the first.

The amount of radical political behavior evidenced at the end of stage three and the beginning of stage four, Incorporation and Handing Over, when power and authority begin to shift to a new generation, reflects both the severity of the long-term effects and the assessment of relocation taken by the younger generations. The more negative the assessment and the more serious the contemporary problem, the greater the chance of radical and violent action. The combination of repressed anger and pain, higher education, and greater awareness of the broader political contexts of local events is a volatile mixture. At Allegany as well as in the Seneca Nation as a whole, the handing over of power to a new generation has resulted in a conservative cultural response, an echo of that demonstrated by the parental generation at the beginning of stage two. The strong emphasis on treaty rights in the current taxation struggle with New York State, the name of the Sovereign Seneka Party (even though the party itself had a brief life), and the desire for closer ties with the Iroquois Confederacy are all indicative of this new posture. It differs, however, from the cultural involution seen in stage two in that it takes a proactive rather than reactive stance and is backed by well-honed political skills and greater economic power.

This brings to the fore an important ethical question about forced relocations. Although most relocated peoples are members of economically and politically powerless groups, some, like the Senecas, are bound to the larger political entity by treaty rights. It is important that national governments recognize both the legal and symbolic importance of these treaties. While treaties have the same legal standing as other laws (i.e., they can be broken or changed), they are perceived by most people as representing a higher moral commitment; they are a pledge of honor between governments. In the words of Supreme Court Justice Hugo Black, writing the minority opinion in the Tuscaroras' losing struggle to stop the New York Power Authority, "Great nations, like great men, should keep their word" (quoted in Ghobashy 1961 and Hauptman 1986a, 1986b). The legacy of distrust resulting from Kinzua Dam continues to impact on relations between the Seneca Nation and state and federal agencies and complicates the efforts of reconciliation by dedicated non-Indian officials.

There were alternatives to the location of Kinzua Dam that would have avoided taking Seneca land and breaking the Canandaigua Treaty. These alternatives would have involved the forced relocation of more people, but people whose right to their property was not guaranteed by treaty. The World Bank's 1990 Operational Directive requires that relocation be avoided or minimized in development projects that it funds. Which, therefore, should take priority, the political rights of indigenous people or the relocation of the smallest number of people, regardless of ethnic, racial, political, or religious status?

To a surprising degree, the experience of the Allegany Senecas presages many of the recommendations for implementation of forced relocations set forth by the World Bank (Cernea 1990; World Bank 1990) in that there was significant community input into the design of the relocation communities and people were able to select the community in which they wanted to live. Rehabilitation funds were used to plan future development, though some plans were ill-advised or unrealistic. The problems that resulted from community participation are related to time constraints. Concern for the social and cultural issues of resettlement occurred long after engineering and economic plans had been finalized, and as a result, the Senecas had a very short period in which to make decisions that would have long-term consequences. If social and engineering plans had been undertaken in conjunction with each other, the long-term economic benefits might have been significant.

If the Senecas at Cattaraugus can be considered analogous to a host community, the provision of rehabilitation funds permitted them access to relocation benefits. Although many researchers have stressed the importance of integrating host communities into the development plans related to resettlements (Salem-Murdock

1993) as a means of reducing host-settler tensions, the Allegany experience suggests that it may also create such tensions, as relocatees may come to resent the fact that others benefited from their losses.

The involvement of the Quakers as a non-government organization (NGO) reflects the use of outside agencies to bring pressure on governments to modify relocation plans. The significant and effective use of the media by the Allegany Senecas and the Quakers is a good illustration of a very early use of this tactic. This cannot be completely attributed to Quaker influence since Iroquois people had gone to the League of Nations early in this century to request international aid in addressing issues of land and human rights.

The relocation model presented by Scudder and Colson remains the "most fruitful" (Partridge 1989, 375) model of the response to forced resettlement. The second stage requires additional analysis in terms of gender and age as well as recognition that all segments of a community (or communities within a large resettlement) may not be in the same stage. The reasons for these differences will vary from case to case, but the model suggests a more homogeneous response than is found. This is probably most true in locales where subsistence is not agriculturally based and wage labor had led to some degree of social stratification. Analysis of the third and, in particular, the fourth stages cannot be fully undertaken until such time as sufficient data show how young people incorporate the fact and meaning of resettlement into their lives and how they translate it into political action. The problem in this regard lies not with the model but with the lack of appropriate data. The Seneca experience strongly suggests that the final stage may result in a surge of political activism and cultural conservatism as the relocated people announce to the surrounding region and state that they will never again be dealt with as a powerless minority.

This case study also indicates that greater attention has to be paid to patterns of descent among dislocated peoples. Comparison of the Allegany Senecas with the Innus and Ojibwas suggests that matrilineality has limited the effects of removal on families by ensuring the continuation of important roles for women and thereby stabilizing family responses. Recent analysis of demographic data from Zambia (Clark, Colson, Lee, and Scudder 1995) shows that descent pattern strongly influences neonatal and child survival and therefore has significant effects on morbidity and mortality levels during stage two. Future research needs to examine the role descent may play in community formation.

The renaming of the stages into more accurate descriptions (Scudder 1997) has advantages over the previous versions of the model, although the first stage would be better called Planning rather than Planning and Recruitment. To speak of "recruits" in involuntary resettlement is an oxymoron. The relocatees are not recruits; they are conscripts.

The fact that the results of relocation can on rare occasions be beneficial, such as the Costa Rican Arenal Hydroelectric Project (Partridge 1993), does not imply that the initial cause for removal was just or necessary, only that the people made the best of a bad situation.

We didn't want to leave. We shouldn't have had to leave. But we wouldn't go back. *—Inez Redeye, June 1987*

Bibliography

Aberle, David F. 1993. The Navajo-Hopi Land Dispute and Navajo Relocation. In *Anthropological Approaches to Resettlement: Policy, Practice, and Theory*, ed. Michael M. Cernea and Scott Guggenheim, 153–200. Boulder CO: Westview.

Abler, Thomas S. 1969. Factional Dispute and Party Conflict in the Political System of the Seneca Nation (1845–1895): An Ethnohistorical Analysis. Ph.D. diss., University of Toronto.

———. 1984. The Kansas Connection: The Seneca Nation and the Iroquois Confederacy Council. In *Extending the Rafters: Interdisciplinary Approaches to Iroquoian Studies*, ed. Michael K. Foster, Jack Campisi, and Marianne Mithun, 81–93. Albany: State University of New York Press.

———. 1992. Protestant Missionaries and Native Culture: Parallel Careers of Asher Wright and Silas T. Rand. *American Indian Quarterly* 16 (1): 25–37.

———. 1997. Personal communication, 28 July.

Abler, Thomas S., and Elisabeth Tooker. 1978. Seneca. In *Northeast*, ed. Bruce G. Trigger, 505–17. Vol. 15 of *Handbook of North American Indians*, ed. William C. Sturtevant. Washington DC: Smithsonian Institution Press.

Ablon, Joan. 1964. Relocated American Indians in the San Francisco Bay Area: Social Interaction and Indian Identity. *Human Organization* 23:296–304.

Abrams, George. 1965. The Cornplanter Cemetery. *Pennsylvania Archaeologist* 35 (pt. 2): 59–73.

158 *Bibliography*

———. 1967. Moving of the Fire: A Case of Iroquois Ritual Innovation. In *Iroquois Culture, History, and Prehistory: Proceedings of the 1965 Conference on Iroquois Research*, 23–24. Albany: University of the State of New York, State Education Department, New York State Museum and Science Service.

———. 1976. *The Seneca People.* Phoenix: Indian Tribal Series.

Ackerman, Lillian, and Laura Klein, eds. 1995. *Women and Power in Native North America.* Norman: University of Oklahoma Press.

Agar, Michael. 1980. *The Professional Stranger: An Informal Approach to Ethnography.* New York: Academic.

Amarteifo, G. W., D. A. P. Butcher, and David Whitham. 1966. *Tema Manhean: A Study of Resettlement.* Accra: Ghana Universities Press.

American Indian Program. 1991. *The Killing of the Waters: Dams, Development and American Indians.* Washington DC: National Museum of American History, Smithsonian Institution.

Apthorpe, Raymond. 1966. *A Survey of Land Resettlement Schemes and Rural Development in East Africa.* Social Sciences Council Conference Paper no. 352. Kampala, Uganda: Makerere Institute of Social Research.

Austin, Alberta. 1986. *Ne'Ho Niyo' De:No': That's What It Was Like*, vol. 1. Lackawanna NY: Rebco Enterprises (published for the Seneca Nation Education Department).

———. 1989. *Ne'Ho Niyo' De:No': That's What It Was Like*, vol. 2. Hamburg NY: Rebco Enterprises (published for the Seneca Nation Education Department).

Behura, N. K., and P. K. Nayak. 1993. Involuntary Displacement and the Changing Frontiers of Kinship: A Study of Resettlement in Orissa. In *Anthropological Approaches to Resettlement: Policy, Practice, and Theory*, ed. Michael M. Cernea and Scott Guggenheim, 283–306. Boulder CO: Westview.

Benedek, Emily. 1993. *The Wind Won't Know Me: A History of the Navajo-Hopi Land Dispute.* New York: Alfred A. Knopf.

Bennett, Robert L. 1961. Building Indian Economies with Land Settlement Funds. *Human Organization* 20:159–63.

Bernard, H. Russell, and Pertti Pelto, eds. 1972. *Technology and Social Change.* New York: Macmillan.

Bilharz, Joy. 1989. The Political Roles of Iroquois Women. Paper presented at the Annual Conference on Iroquois Research, 14 October, Rensselaerville NY.

———. 1995. First among Equals? The Changing Status of Seneca Women. In *Women and Power in Native North America*, ed. Lillian Ackerman and Laura Klein, 101–12. Norman: University of Oklahoma Press.

———. 1996. Fieldnotes, June, Akwesasne.

Bilharz, Joy, and Thomas Abler. 1996. Kinzua's Legacy: Women and Seneca Nation Politics. Paper presented at the 95th Annual Meeting of the American Anthropological Association, 24 November, San Francisco.

Bonvillain, Nancy. 1980. Iroquoian Women. In *Studies on Iroquoian Culture*, ed. Nancy Bonvillain, 47–58. Occasional Papers in Northeastern Anthropology no. 6. Peterborough NH: Peterborough Transcript.

Borup, Jerry H., Daniel T. Gallego, and Pamela G. Heffernan. 1979. Relocation and Its Effect on Mortality. *Gerontologist* 19 (2): 135–40.

Brand, Daniel. 1984. Outward Bound: The Transportation Assumptions of Crisis Relocation Planning. In *The Counterfeit Ark: Crisis Relocation for Nuclear War*, ed. Jennifer Leaning and Langley Keyes, 79–117. Cambridge MA: Ballinger.

Brant, Roy E. 1970. A Flood Control Dam for the Upper Allegheny River: Forty Years of Controversy. Ph.D. diss., University of Pittsburgh.

Brinker, Paul A., and Benjamin J. Taylor. 1974. Southern Plains Indian Relocation Returnees. *Human Organization* 33:139–46.

Brokensha, David. 1965. Volta Resettlement and Anthropological Research. *Human Organization* 2:286–90.

Brokensha, David, and Marion Pearsall, eds. 1969. *The Anthropology of Development in Sub-Saharan Africa.* Society for Applied Anthropology, Monograph no. 10. Lexington: University Press of Kentucky (published for the Society for Applied Anthropology).

Brokensha, David, and Thayer Scudder. 1968. Resettlement. In *Dams in Africa: An Inter-disciplinary Study of Man-Made Lakes in Africa*, ed. Neville Rubin and William M. Warren, 20–62. New York: Augustus M. Kelley.

Broom, Leonard, and John I. Kitsuse. 1956. *The Managed Casualty: The Japanese-American Family in World War II.* Berkeley: University of California Press.

Broom, Leonard, and Ruth Riemer. 1949. *Removal and Return: The Socio-economic Effects of the War on Japanese Americans.* University of California Publications in Culture and Society no. 4.

Brown, Judith K. 1970. Economic Organization and the Position of Women among the Iroquois. *Ethnohistory* 17:151–67.

Butterworth, Douglas. 1980. *The People of Buena Ventura: Relocation of Slum Dwellers in Postrevolutionary Cuba.* Urbana: University of Illinois Press.

Campbell, Richard Dean. 1985. *The People of the Land of Flint.* Lanham MD: University Press of America.

Campisi, Jack. 1984. National Policy, States' Rights, and Indian Sovereignty: The Case of the New York Iroquois. In *Extending the Rafters: Interdisciplinary Approaches to Iroquoian Studies,* ed. Michael K. Foster, Jack Campisi, and Marianne Mithun, 98–108. Albany: State University of New York Press.

Cernea, Michael M. 1990. From Unused Social Knowledge to Policy Creation: The Case of Population Resettlement. Development Discussion Paper no. 342. Cambridge: Harvard Institute for International Development.

———. 1991a. Knowledge from Social Science for Development Policies and Projects. In *Putting People First: Sociological Variables in Rural Development,* 2d ed., ed. Michael M. Cernea, 1–41. London: Oxford University Press.

———. 1991b. Involuntary Resettlement: Social Research, Policy, and Planning. In *Putting People First: Sociological Variables in Rural Development,* 2d ed., ed. Michael M. Cernea, 188–215. London: Oxford University Press.

———. 1993a. Anthropological and Sociological Research for Policy Development on Population Resettlement. In *Anthropological Approaches to Resettlement: Policy, Practice, and Theory,* ed. Michael M. Cernea and Scott Guggenheim, 13–38. Boulder CO: Westview.

———. 1993b. Disaster-Related Refugee Flows and Development-Caused Population Displacement. In *Anthropological Approaches* to *Resettlement: Policy, Practice, and Theory,* ed. Michael M. Cernea and Scott Guggenheim, 375–402. Boulder CO: Westview.

Cernea, Michael M., and Scott Guggenheim. 1994. *Resettlement and Development: The Bankwide Review of Projects Involving Involuntary Resettlement, 1986–1993.* Washington DC: World Bank, Environment Department.

Cernea, Michael M., and Scott Guggenheim, eds. 1993. *Anthropological Approaches to Resettlement: Policy, Practice, and Theory.* Boulder CO: Westview.

Chadwick, Bruce A., and Joseph H. Stauss. 1975. The Assimilation of American Indians into Urban Society: The Seattle Case. *Human Organization* 34:359–69.

Chambers, Robert. 1991. Shortcut and Participatory Methods for Gaining Social Information for Projects. In *Putting People First: Sociological Variables in Rural Development,* 2d ed., ed. Michael M. Cernea, 515–37. London: Oxford University Press.

Chazanof, William. 1970. *Joseph Ellicott and the Holland Land Company.* Syracuse NY: Syracuse University Press.

Clark, Sam, Elizabeth Colson, James Lee, and Thayer Scudder. 1995. Ten Thousand Tonga: A Longitudinal Anthropological Study from Southern Zambia. *Population Studies* 49:91–109.

Coles, Robert. 1970. *Uprooted Children: The Early Life of Migrant Farm Workers.* Pittsburgh: University of Pittsburgh Press.

———. 1986. *The Political Life of Children: The Early Life of Migrant Farm Workers.* Pittsburgh: University of Pittsburgh Press.

Colson, Elisabeth. 1971. *The Social Consequences of Resettlement: The Impact of the Kariba Resettlement upon the Gwembe Tonga.* Kariba Studies no. 4. Manchester: Manchester University Press.

Congdon, Charles E. 1967. *Allegany Oxbow: A History of Allegany State Park and the Allegany Reserve of the Seneca Nation.* Little Valley NY: Straight.

Cornplanter Descendants Association. Papers. Reed Library, State University of New York, College at Fredonia.

Cornplanter Tribe Asks State Archeological Group to Halt Dam Plan. 1935. *Pennsylvania Archaeologist* 5 (3): 66.

Davis, Shelton H. 1993. The World Bank and Indigenous Peoples. Paper prepared for panel discussion, Indigenous Peoples and Ethnic Minorities, at the Denver Initiative Conference on Human Rights, 16–17 April, University of Denver Law School, Denver.

Davis, Shelton H., and Lars T. Soeftestad. 1995. Participation and Indigenous Peoples. Participation Series, no. 021. Washington DC: World Bank, Environment Department.

Dean, Michelle. 1983. Personal communication, October.

Deardorff, Merle H. 1941. The Cornplanter Grant in Warren County. *Western Pennsylvania Historical Magazine* 24 (1): 1–22.

———. 1951. The Religion of Handsome Lake: Its Origin and Development. *Bureau of American Ethnology Bulletin* 149 (5): 77–107.

———. Papers. MG 220. Pennsylvania State Archives, Harrisburg.

Deardorff, Merle H., and George S. Snyderman, eds. 1956. A Nineteenth-Century Journal of a Visit to the Indians of New York. *Proceedings of the American Philosophical Society* 100 (6): 582–612.

DeMont, John. 1994. The Fight of a Lifetime. *Maclean's*, 17 January, 20–26.

de Wet, Chris. 1993. A Spatial Analysis of Involuntary Community Relocation: A South African Case Study. In *Anthropological Approaches to Resettlement: Policy, Practice, and Theory*, ed. Michael M. Cernea and Scott Guggenheim, 321–50. Boulder CO: Westview.

Diamond, Stanley, William C. Sturtevant, and William N. Fenton. 1964. Memorandum Submitted to Subcommittees on Indian Affairs of the Senate and House of Representatives. *American Anthropologist* 66:631–33.

Eckert, J. Kevin. 1983. Dislocation and Relocation of the Urban Elderly: Social Networks as Mediators of Relocation Stress. *Human Organization* 42:39–45.

Epstein, Helen. 1979. *Children of the Holocaust: Conversations with Sons and Daughters of Survivors.* Toronto: Bantam.

Erikson, Kai T. 1976. *Everything in Its Path: Destruction of Community in the Buffalo Creek Flood.* New York: Simon and Schuster.

Euler, Robert C., and Henry F. Dobyns. 1961. Ethnic Group Land Rights in the Modern State: Three Case Studies. *Human Organization* 2:302–7.

Fahim, Hussein M. 1983. *Egyptian Nubians: Resettlement and Years of Coping.* Salt Lake City: University of Utah Press.

Farrer, Claire R. 1996. *Thunder Rides a Black Horse: Mescalero Apaches and the Mythic Present,* 2d ed. Prospect Heights IL: Waveland.

Feldsher, Paul. 1970. The Effects of the Kinzua Dam upon Seneca Culture. MG 220, Box 4. Pennsylvania State Archives, Harrisburg.

Feldsher, Paul, and Susan Williams, eds. 1972. Sociological Impact of a Radical Environmental Change on a Group of Seneca Indians. Syracuse University. Mimeographed.

Fellows, Zoe. 1982. Achievement, Ability, and the Indian Dropout in the Salamanca Schools. Department of Education, Seneca Nation of Indians. Mimeographed.

Fenton, William N. 1936. *An Outline of Seneca Ceremonies at Coldspring Longhouse.* Publication in Anthropology no. 9. New Haven: Yale University. Reprint, New Haven CT: Human Relations Area Files, 1970.

———. 1941. Iroquois Suicide: A Study in the Stability of a Culture Pattern. *Bureau of American Ethnology Bulletin* 128:88–137.

———. 1945–46. Place Names and Related Activities of the Cornplanter Senecas. *Pennsylvania Archaeologist* 15:25–29, 42–50, 88–96, 108–18; 16:42–57.

———. 1951. Locality as a Basic Factor in the Development of Iroquois Social Structure. *Bureau of American Ethnology Bulletin* 149 (3): 37–54.

———. 1957. Long-Term Trends of Change among the Iroquois. In *Cultural Stability and Culture Change,* ed. Verne F. Ray, 30–35. Proceedings of the 1957 Annual Meeting of the American Ethnological Society. Seattle: University of Washington Press.

———. 1960. Letter to Rep. James Haley, Chair, House Subcommittee on Indian Affairs, 4 July.

———. 1967. From Longhouse to Ranch-Type House: The Second Housing Revolution of the Seneca Nation. In *Iroquois Culture, History, and Prehistory,* ed. Elisabeth Tooker, 7–22. Proceedings of the 1965 Conference on Iroquois Research. Albany: University of the State of New York, State Education Department, New York State Museum and Science Service.

———. 1972. The Iroquois Confederacy in the Twentieth Century: A Case Study of the Theory of Lewis Henry Morgan in *Ancient*

Society. In *The Emergent Native Americans: A Reader in Culture Contact*, ed. Deward E. Walker Jr., 471–84. Boston: Little, Brown.

———. 1985a. Personal communication, October, Rensselaerville NY.

———. 1985b. Structure, Continuity, and Change in the Process of Iroquois Treaty Making. In *The History and Culture of Iroquois Diplomacy: An Interdisciplinary Guide to the Treaties of the Six Nations and Their League*, ed. Francis Jennings, 37–65. Syracuse NY: Syracuse University Press.

———. 1986. A Further Note on Iroquois Suicide. *Ethnohistory* 33:448–57.

———. 1987. *The False Faces of the Iroquois.* Norman: University of Oklahoma Press.

———. 1991. *The Iroquois Eagle Dance: An Offshoot of the Calumet Dance.* Syracuse NY: Syracuse University Press.

Fenton, William N., ed. 1965. The Journal of James Emlen Kept on a Trip to Canandaigua, New York, September 15 to October 30, 1794, to Attend the Treaty between the United States and the Six Nations. *Ethnohistory* 12:279–342.

———, ed. 1968. *Parker on the Iroquois.* Syracuse NY: Syracuse University Press.

Fernea, Robert A., and John G. Kennedy. 1966. Initial Adaptations to Resettlement: A New Life for Egyptian Nubians. *Current Anthropology* 7:349–54.

Fixico, Donald L. 1986. *Termination and Relocation: Federal Indian Policy, 1945–1960.* Albuquerque: University of New Mexico Press.

Foreman, Grant. 1934. *The Five Civilized Tribes.* Norman: University of Oklahoma Press.

———. 1946. *The Last Trek of the Indians.* New York: Russell and Russell.

———. 1953. *Indian Removal: The Emigration of the Five Civilized Tribes of Indians.* Norman: University of Oklahoma Press.

Foster, George M., Thayer Scudder, Elisabeth Colson, and Robert V. Kemper, eds. 1979. *Long-Term Field Research in Social Anthropology.* New York: Academic.

Foster, Michael, Jack Campisi, and Marianne Mithun, eds. 1984. *Ex-*

tending the Rafters: Interdisciplinary Approaches to Iroquoian Studies. Albany: State University of New York Press.

Frideres, J., J. DiSanto, S. Goldenberg, and U. Fleising. 1985. The Keephills Hamlet Relocation. *Practicing Anthropology* 7 (3): 13–14, 16.

Fried, Marc. 1963. Grieving for a Lost Home. In *The Urban Condition: People and Policy in the Metropolis*, ed. Leonard J. Duhl, 151–71. New York: Basic Books.

Fuhriman, Walter U. 1963. *Seneca Indians Who Will Be Affected by the Kinzua Dam Reservoir*. Missouri River Basin Investigations Project, Report no. 175. Billings MT: Bureau of Indian Affairs, U.S. Department of the Interior.

Garbarino, Merwyn. 1971. Life in the City: Chicago. In *The American Indian in Urban Society*, ed. Jack O. Waddell and O. Michael Watson, 168–205. Boston: Little, Brown.

Geiser, Peter. 1973. The Myth of the Dam. *American Anthropologist* 75:184–94.

Ghobashy, Omar Z. 1961. *The Caughnawaga Indians and the St. Lawrence Seaway*. New York: Devin-Adair.

Gibson, John Arthur. 1992. *Concerning the League: The Iroquois League Tradition as Dictated in Onondaga by John Arthur Gibson; edited and translated by Hanni Woodbury; in collaboration with Reg Henry and Harry Webster; on the basis of A. A. Goldenweiser's manuscript*. Memoir no. 9. Winnipeg MB: Algonquian and Iroquoian Linguistics.

Gilmour, David. 1980. *Dispossessed: The Ordeal of the Palestinians, 1917–1980*. London: Sidgwick and Jackson.

Goldsmith, Edward, and Nicholas Hildyard. 1987. *The Social and Environmental Effects of Large Dams*. San Francisco: Sierra Club.

Graves, Theodore. 1966. Alternative Models for the Study of Urban Migration. *Human Organization* 25:195–99.

———. 1971. Drinking and Drunkenness among American Indians. In *The American Indian in Urban Society*, ed. Jack O. Waddell and O. Michael Watson, 274–311. Boston: Little, Brown.

Graves, Theodore D., and Minor Van Arsdale. 1966. Values, Expectations and Relocation: The Navajo Migrant to Denver. *Human Organization* 25:300–307.

Gray, John. 1997a. Nightmare of Davis Inlet Haunting Innu Dreams. *Globe and Mail* (Toronto), 31 March.

———. 1997b. Innu Fear the Impact of Voisey's Bay. *Globe and Mail* (Toronto), 1 April.

Graymont, Barbara. 1972. *The Iroquois in the American Revolution*. Syracuse NY: Syracuse University Press.

Green, Michael D. 1982. *The Politics of Indian Removal: Creek Government and Society in Crisis*. Lincoln: University of Nebraska Press.

Griffen, Joyce. 1981. My Mother, Myself, My Daughter: The Case of the Urban Navajo Woman. Paper presented at the Western Social Science Association Convention, San Diego. Mimeographed.

Guggenheim, Scott. 1994. *Involuntary Resettlement: An Annotated Reference Bibliography for Development Research*. Environment Working Paper no. 64. Washington DC: Environment Department, World Bank.

Guillemin, Jeanne. 1975. *Urban Renegades: The Cultural Strategies of American Indians*. New York: Columbia University Press.

Hansen, Art. 1982. Self-Settled Rural Refugees in Africa: The Case of Angolans in Zambian Villages. In *Involuntary Migration and Resettlement: The Problems and Responses of Dislocated People*, ed. Art Hansen and Anthony Oliver-Smith, 13–35. Boulder CO: Westview.

Hansen, Art, and Anthony Oliver-Smith, eds. 1982. *Involuntary Migration and Resettlement: The Problems and Responses of Dislocated People*. Boulder CO: Westview.

Harbeson, John W. 1967. Land Settlement and Development Strategy in Kenya. Social Sciences Council Conference Paper no. 437. Makerere Institute of Social Research, Kampala, Uganda. Mimeographed.

Hauptman, Laurence. 1980. Refugee Havens: The Iroquois Villages of the Eighteenth Century. In *American Indian Environments: Ecological Issues in Native American History*, ed. Christopher Vecsey and Robert W. Venables, 128–39. Syracuse NY: Syracuse University Press.

———. 1981. *The Iroquois and the New Deal*. Syracuse NY: Syracuse University Press.

———. 1986a. *The Iroquois Struggle for Survival: World War II to the Emergence of Red Power.* Syracuse NY: Syracuse University Press.

———. 1986b. General John S. Bragdon, the Office of Public Works Planning, and the Decision to Build Pennsylvania's Kinzua Dam. *Pennsylvania History* 53:181–200.

———. 1988. *Formulating American Indian Policy in New York State, 1970–1986.* Albany: State University of New York Press.

Heller, Tamar. 1982. The Effects of Involuntary Residential Relocation: A Review. *American Journal of Community Psychology* 10 (4): 471–92.

Hersey, John. 1946. *Hiroshima.* New York: Alfred A. Knopf.

Hertzberg, Hazel W. 1966. *The Great Tree and the Longhouse: The Culture of the Iroquois.* New York: Macmillan.

———. 1971. *The Search for an American Indian Identity: Modern Pan-Indian Movements.* Syracuse NY: Syracuse University Press.

———. 1986. Personal communication, 4 October, Rensselaerville NY.

Hodge, William H. 1971. Navajo Urban Migration: An Analysis from the Perspective of the Family. In *The American Indian in Urban Society*, ed. Jack O. Waddell and O. Michael Watson, 346–91. Boston: Little, Brown.

Hogan, Thomas E. 1974a. A History of the Allegany Reservation: 1850–1900. Master's thesis, State University of New York, College at Fredonia.

———. 1974b. City in a Quandary: Salamanca and the Allegany Leases. *New York History* 55:79–101.

Horowitz, Michael M., Dolores Koenig, Curt Grimm, and Yacouba Konate. 1993. Resettlement at Manantali, Mali: Short-Term Success, Long-Term Problems. In *Anthropological Approaches to Resettlement: Policy, Practice, and Theory*, ed. Michael M. Cernea and Scott Guggenheim, 229–50. Boulder CO: Westview.

Howarth, David. 1961. *The Shadow of the Dam.* New York: Macmillan.

Hunt, George. 1940. *The Wars of the Iroquois: A Study of Intertribal Trade Relations.* Madison: University of Wisconsin Press.

Hurt, Wesley R., Jr. 1961. The Urbanization of Yankton Indians. *Human Organization* 21:226–31.

Ingersoll, Jasper. 1968. Mekong River Basin Development: Anthropology in a New Setting. *Anthropological Quarterly* 41:147–67.

Jackson, Halliday. 1806. Some Account of a Visit Paid to the Friends at Tunesassa and the Indians Living on Allegany and Cattaraugus Rivers, Agreeably—to an Appointment by the Committee on Indian Affairs in the 8th Month 1806. Typescript by Merle H. Deardorff of original microfilm. MG 220, Pennsylvania State Archives, Harrisburg.

James, Sydney V. 1963. *A People among Peoples: Quaker Benevolence in Eighteenth-Century America.* Cambridge: Harvard University Press.

Jennings, Francis. 1984. *The Ambiguous Iroquois Empire: The Covenant Chain Confederation of Indian Tribes with English Colonies from Its Beginnings to the Lancaster Treaty of 1744.* New York: W. W. Norton.

———. 1985a. Iroquois Alliances in American History. In *The History and Culture of Iroquois Diplomacy: An Interdisciplinary Guide to the Treaties of the Six Nations and Their League,* ed. Francis Jennings, 37–65. Syracuse NY: Syracuse University Press.

Jennings, Francis, ed. 1985b. *The History and Culture of Iroquois Diplomacy: An Interdisciplinary Guide to the Treaties of the Six Nations and Their League.* Syracuse NY: Syracuse University Press.

John, Randy. 1989. Social Integration of an Elderly Native American Population: The Allegany Seneca Elders. Ph.D. diss., Syracuse University.

Jordan, Janet E., ed. 1982. Transcript of Hearings Held by the Navajo Nation on Effects of Relocation on Navajos Who Have Relocated from the Joint Use Area. Coconino County Courthouse, Flagstaff AZ, 6 May. Mimeographed.

Josephy, Alvin M., Jr. 1982. *Now That the Buffalo's Gone: A Study of Today's American Indians.* New York: Alfred A. Knopf.

Katarikawa, E. 1966. Some Preliminary Results of a Survey of Kiga Resettlement Schemes in Kigezi, Ankole and Toro Districts, Western Uganda. Rural Development Research Project Paper no. 31. Makerere Institute of Social Research, Kampala, Uganda. Mimeographed.

Kearney, Michael. 1986. From the Invisible Hand to Visible Feet: Anthropological Studies of Migration and Development. In *Annual Review of Anthropology* 15, ed. Bernard J. Siegel, 331–61. Palo Alto CA: Annual Reviews.

Kent, Donald H. 1974a. *Iroquois Indians*. Vol. 1, *History of Pennsylvania Purchases from the Indians*. New York: Garland.

———. 1974b. *Iroquois Indians*. Vol. 2, *Historical Report on the Niagara River and the Niagara River Strip to* 1759, and Commission Findings (Indian Claims Commission). New York: Garland.

———. Papers. Pennsylvania State Archives, Harrisburg.

Kent, Donald K., and Merle H. Deardorff. 1960. John Adlum on the Allegheny: Memoirs for the Year 1794. *Pennsylvania Magazine of History and Biography* 84:265–324, 435–80.

Khera, Sigrid, and Patricia S. Mariella. 1982. The Fort McDowell Yavapai: A Case of Long-Term Resistance to Relocation. In *Involuntary Migration and Resettlement: The Problems and Responses of Dislocated People*, ed. Art Hansen and Anthony Oliver-Smith, 159–77. Boulder CO: Westview.

Kiste, Robert. 1972. Relocation and Technological Change in Micronesia. In *Technology and Social Change*, ed. H. Russell Bernard and Pertti Pelto, 71–107. New York: Macmillan.

———. 1974. *The Bikinians: A Study in Forced Migration*. Menlo Park CA: Cummings.

Klein, Philip S., and Ari Hoogenboom. 1980. *A History of Pennsylvania*, 2d ed. University Park: Pennsylvania State University Press.

Kolb, Joy Bilharz. 1985. Relocation as Process: The Allegany Senecas after Kinzua Dam. Paper presented at the Annual Conference on Iroquois Research, 12 October, Rensselaerville NY.

Kottak, Conrad Phillip. 1991. When People Don't Come First: Some Sociological Lessons from Completed Projects. In *Putting People First: Sociological Variables in Rural Development*, 2d ed., ed. Michael M. Cernea, 431–64. London: Oxford University Press.

Krotz, Larry. 1980. *Urban Indians: The Strangers in Canada's Cities*. Edmonton: Hurtig.

LaFarge, Peter. 1964. As Long As the Grass Shall Grow. Performed by Johnny Cash, *Bitter Tears*, Columbia CS 9048.

Landsman, Gail. 1985. Ganienkeh: Symbol and Politics in an Indian/White Conflict. *American Anthropologist* 87:826–39.

————. 1986. Personal communication, 4 October, Rensselaerville
    NY.

Langness, L. L., and Gelya Frank. 1981. *Lives: An Anthropological
    Approach to Biography.* Novato CA: Chandler and Sharp.

Lavin, Chris. 1985. The Iroquois: A People Apart. *Rochester Times-
    Union,* October, Special Reprint.

Lawson, Michael. 1982. *Damned Indians: The Pick-Sloan Plan and
    the Missouri River Sioux, 1944–1980.* Norman: University of
    Oklahoma Press.

Leacock, Eleanor. 1978. Women's Status in Egalitarian Societies.
    Current Anthropology 19 (2): 247–54, 268–75.

Leaning, Jennifer, and Langley Keyes, eds. 1984. *The Counterfeit
    Ark: Crisis Relocation for Nuclear War.* Cambridge MA: Bal-
    linger.

Lifton, Robert Jay. 1967. *Death in Life: Survivors of Hiroshima.*
    New York: Random House.

Lifton, Robert Jay, Eric Markusen, and Dorothy Austin. 1984. The
    Second Death: Psychological Survival after Nuclear War. In *The
    Counterfeit Ark: Crisis Relocation for Nuclear War,* ed. Jennifer
    Leaning and Langley Keyes, 285–300. Cambridge MA: Ballinger.

Lipsky, Michael. 1984. Things Fall Apart: Problems of Governance
    and Social Control. In *The Counterfeit Ark: Crisis Relocation
    for Nuclear War,* ed. Jennifer Leaning and Langley Keyes, 144–58.
    Cambridge MA: Ballinger.

Maclean, Charles. 1972. *Island on the Edge of the World: The Story
    of St. Kilda.* Edinburgh: Canongate.

Madigan, LaVerne. 1956. *The American Indian Relocation Pro-
    gram.* New York: Association of American Indian Affairs.

Mann, Michael. 1973. *Workers on the Move: The Sociology of Re-
    location.* Cambridge: Cambridge University Press.

Martin, Harry W. 1964. Correlates of Adjustment among American In-
    dians in an Urban Environment. *Human Organization* 23:290–95.

Mason, Leonard. 1950. The Bikinians: A Transplanted Population.
    Human Organization 9:5–15.

Maynard, Eileen. 1974. The Growing Negative Image of the Anthro-
    pologist among American Indians. *Human Organization*
    33:402–4.

McConnell, Michael N. 1992. *A Country Between: The Upper*

Ohio Valley and Its Peoples, 1724–1774. Lincoln: University of Nebraska Press.

McElwain, Thomas. 1978. *Mythological Tales and the Allegany Seneca*. Stockholm Studies in Comparative Religion no. 17. Stockholm: Almqvists and Wiksell International.

Mele, A. Lucia. 1984. The Seneca Nation of Indians and the City of Salamanca: An Analysis of the Senecas' Options for Renewal of the 99-Year Leases of Salamanca. Master's thesis, Massachusetts Institute of Technology.

Miner, Horace. 1960. Culture Change under Pressure: A Hausa Case. *Human Organization* 19:164–67.

Mithun, Jacqueline S. 1975. Cooperative Community Solidarity against Urban Renewal. *Human Organization* 34:79–86.

Morgan, Arthur E. 1971. *Dams and Other Disasters: A Century of the Army Corps of Engineers in Civil Works*. Boston: Porter Sargent.

Morgan, Lewis Henry. 1962 [1851]. *League of the Iroquois*. Seacaucus NJ: Citadel.

Morrison, G. S., and Felix Moos. 1982. Halfway to Nowhere: Vietnamese Refugees on Guam. In *Involuntary Migration and Resettlement: The Problems and Responses of Dislocated People*, ed. Art Hansen and Anthony Oliver-Smith, 49–68. Boulder CO: Westview.

Nagata, Shuichi. 1971. The Reservation Community and the Urban Community: Hopi Indians of Moenkopi. In *The American Indian in Urban Society*, ed. Jack O. Waddell and O. Michael Watson, 114–59. Boston: Little, Brown.

Naroll, Raoul, and Ronald Cohen, eds. 1970. *A Handbook of Method in Cultural Anthropology*. New York: Columbia University Press.

Natelson Company. 1981. An Investigation of Costs Associated with the Implementation of Public Law 93–531. Interim Report, 15 May. Mimeographed.

Navajo and Hopi Indian Relocation Commission. 1978. *Interim Progress Report*. Washington DC: U.S. Government Printing Office.

———. 1980. Annual Report no. 5. Flagstaff AZ: Navajo and Hopi Indian Relocation Commission.

———. 1981. Report and Plan. Flagstaff AZ: Navajo and Hopi Indian Relocation Commission.

————. 1982. Land Selection and Transfer Progress Report: Public
Law 93–531, As Amended. Annual Report no. 2. Flagstaff AZ: Navajo and Hopi Indian Relocation Commission.

Noon, John A. 1949. *Law and Government of the Grand River Iroquois.* Viking Fund Publications in Anthropology no. 12.

Oliver-Smith, Anthony. 1982. Here There Is Life: The Social and Cultural Dynamics of Successful Resistance to Resettlement in
Postdisaster Peru. In *Involuntary Migration and Resettlement:
The Problems and Responses of Dislocated People,* ed. Art Hansen and Anthony Oliver-Smith, 85–103. Boulder CO: Westview.

————. 1986. *The Martyred City. Death and Rebirth in the Andes.*
Albuquerque: University of New Mexico Press.

————. 1991. Involuntary Resettlement, Resistance and Political
Empowerment. *Journal of Refugee Studies* 4 (2): 132–49.

Oliver-Smith, Anthony, and Art Hansen. 1982. Involuntary Migration and Resettlement: Causes and Contexts. In *Involuntary Migration and Resettlement: The Problems and Responses of Dislocated People,* ed. Art Hansen and Anthony Oliver-Smith, 1–9.
Boulder CO: Westview.

Olson, John W. 1971. Epilogue: The Urban Indian as Viewed by an
Indian Caseworker. In *The American Indian in Urban Society,*
ed. Jack O. Waddell and O. Michael Watson, 398–408. Boston:
Little, Brown.

Otten, Mariel. 1986. *Transmigrasi: Myths and Realities. Indonesian Resettlement Policy, 1965–1985.* Document no. 57.
Copenhagen: International Work Group for Indigenous Affairs.

Paine, Robert. 1982. *Dam a River, Damn a People? Saami (Lapp)
Livelihood and the Alta/Kautokeino Hydro-electric Project and
the Norwegian Parliament.* Document no. 45. Copenhagen: International Work Group for Indigenous Affairs.

Palmer, Gary. 1974. The Ecology of Resettlement Schemes. *Human
Organization* 33:239–50.

Parker, Arthur C. 1968. The Iroquois Constitution. In *Parker on the
Iroquois,* ed. William N. Fenton, 7–13. Syracuse NY: Syracuse
University Press.

Partridge, William L. 1989. Involuntary Resettlement in Development Projects. *Journal of Refugee Studies* 2 (3): 373–84.

———. 1993. Successful Involuntary Resettlement: Lessons from the Costa Rican Arenal Hydroelectric Project. In *Anthropological Approaches to Resettlement: Policy, Practice, and Theory*, ed. Michael M. Cernea and Scott Guggeheim, 351–74. Boulder CO: Westview.

Partridge, William L., Antoinette B. Brown, and Jeffrey B. Nugent. 1982. The Papaloapan Dam and Resettlement Project: Human Ecology and Health Impacts. In *Involuntary Migration and Resettlement: Problems and Responses of Dislocated People*, ed. Art Hansen and Anthony Oliver-Smith, 246–63. Boulder CO: Westview.

Perlman, Janice E. 1982. Favela Removal: The Eradication of a Lifestyle. In *Involuntary Migration and Resettlement: The Problems and Responses of Dislocated People*, ed. Art Hansen and Anthony Oliver-Smith, 225–43. Boulder CO: Westview.

Petersen, Marie-Louise Deth. 1986. The Impact of Public Planning on Ethnic Culture: Aspects of Danish Resettlement Policies in Greenland after World War II. *Arctic Anthropology* 23:271–80.

Peterson, John H., Jr. 1972. Assimilation, Separation, and Out-Migration in an American Indian Group. *American Anthropologist* 74:1286–94.

Philadelphia Yearly Meeting of Friends. 1961. *The Kinzua Dam Controversy: A Practical Solution—Without Shame*. Philadelphia: Kinzua Project of the Indian Committee of the Philadelphia Yearly Meeting of Friends.

Pisarowicz, James A., and Vicki Tosher. 1982. Vietnamese Refugee Resettlement: Denver, Colorado, 1975–1977. In *Involuntary Migration and Resettlement: The Problems and Responses of Dislocated People*, ed. Art Hansen and Anthony Oliver-Smith, 69–81. Boulder CO: Westview.

Platzky, Laurine, and Cheryl Walker. 1986. *The Surplus People: Forced Removals in South Africa*. Johannesburg: Ravan.

Posluns, Michael. 1993. *Voices from the Odeyak*. Toronto: NC Press.

Price, John A. 1968. The Migration and Adaptation of American Indians to Los Angeles. *Human Organization* 27:168–75.

———. 1978. *Native Studies: American and Canadian Indians*. Toronto: McGraw-Hill Ryerson.

Prucha, Francis Paul. 1962. *American Indian Policy in the Formative Years: The Indian Trade and Intercourse Acts.* Lincoln: University of Nebraska Press.

Randle, Martha Champion. 1951. Iroquois Women, Then and Now. *Bureau of American Ethnology Bulletin* 149 (8): 167–80.

Reining, Conrad. 1982. Resettlement in the Zande Development Scheme. In *Involuntary Migration and Resettlement: Problems and Responses of Dislocated People*, ed. Art Hansen and Anthony Oliver-Smith, 201–24. Boulder CO: Westview.

Report of the Committee for the Gradual Civilization of the Indian Natives, Made to the Yearly Meeting of the Religious Society of Friends, Held in Philadelphia, in the Fourth Month, 1838. 1838. Philadelphia: Joseph and William Kite.

Richards, Cara. 1957. Matriarchy or Mistake: The Role of Iroquois Women through Time. In *Cultural Stability and Cultural Change*, ed. Verne F. Ray, 36–45. Proceedings of the 1957 Annual Meeting of the American Ethnology Society. Seattle: University of Washington Press.

———. 1974. Onondaga Women: Among the Liberated. In *Many Sisters: Women in Cross-Cultural Perspective*, ed. Carolyn J. Matthiasson, 401–19. New York: Free Press.

Richling, Barnett. 1985. Stuck Up on a Rock: Resettlement and Community Development in Hopedale, Labrador. *Human Organization* 44:348–53.

Richter, Daniel K. 1983. War and Culture: The Iroquois Experience. *William and Mary Quarterly*, 3d ser., 40:528–59.

———. 1992. *The Ordeal of the Longhouse: The Peoples of the Iroquois League in the Era of European Colonialism.* Chapel Hill: University of North Carolina Press.

Robertson, Ian. 1981. *Sociology*, 2d ed. New York: Wirth.

Rothenberg, Diane. 1976. Friends Like These: An Ethnohistorical Analysis of the Interaction between Allegheny Senecas and Quakers, 1798–1823. Ph.D. diss., City University of New York.

———. 1980. The Mothers of the Nation: Seneca Resistance to Quaker Intervention. In *Women and Colonization: Anthropological Perspectives*, ed. Mona Etienne and Eleanor Leacock, 63–87. New York: Praeger.

———. 1986a. Personal communication, October, Rensselaerville NY.

————. 1986b. On the Insanity of Cornplanter. Paper presented at the 85th Annual Meeting of the American Anthropological Association, December, Philadelphia.

————. N.d. Property and People: Inheritance as Adaptation. Mimeographed.

Rubin, Neville, and William M. Warren, eds. 1968. *Dams in Africa: An Inter-disciplinary Study of Man-Made Lakes in Africa.* New York: Augustus M. Kelley.

Safran, Franciska. 1986. The Indian Reservations on the Holland Purchase. Paper delivered at the Seneca-Iroquois National Museum, 6 September, Salamanca NY.

Sainte-Marie, Buffy. 1970a. *My Country 'Tis of Thy People You're Dying.* Gypsy Boy Music, ASCAP.

————. 1970b. *Now That the Buffalo's Gone.* Gypsy Boy Music, ASCAP.

Salem-Murdock, Muneera. 1993. Involuntary Resettlement: A Plea for the Host Population. In *Anthropological Approaches to Resettlement: Policy, Practice, and Theory,* ed. Michael M. Cernea and Scott Guggenheim, 307–20. Boulder CO: Westview.

Satz, Ronald N. 1975. *American Indian Policy in the Jacksonian Era.* Lincoln: University of Nebraska Press.

Savery, William. 1844. A Journal of the Life, Travels, and Religious Labors of William Savery, a Minister of the Gospel of Christ, of the Society of Friends, Late of Philadelphia. Compiled from his original memoranda by Jonathan Evans. Philadelphia: Friends' Book-Store.

Sayigh, Rosemary. 1979. *Palestinians: From Peasants to Revolutionaries.* London: Zed.

Schoepfle, Mark, Michael Burton, and Frank Morgan. 1984. Navajos and Energy Development: Economic Decision Making under Political Uncertainty. *Human Organization* 43:265–76.

Scudder, Thayer. 1965. The Kariba Case: Manmade Lakes and Resource Development in Africa. *Bulletin of the Atomic Scientists* 21:6–11.

————. 1968. Social Anthropology, Man-Made Lakes and Population Relocation in Africa. *Anthropological Quarterly* 41:168–76.

————. 1969. Relocation, Agricultural Intensification, and Anthropological Research. In *The Anthropology of Development in*

Sub-Saharan Africa, ed. David Brokensha and Marion Pearsall, 31–39. Society for Applied Anthropology, Monograph no. 10. Lexington: University Press of Kentucky (published for the Society for Applied Anthropology).

———. 1973. The Human Ecology of Big Projects: River Basin Development and Resettlement. *Annual Review of Anthropology* 2:45–61.

———. 1982. *No Place to Go: Effects of Compulsory Relocation on Navajos*. Philadelphia: Institute for the Study of Human Issues.

———. 1991. A Sociological Framework for the Analysis of New Land Settlements. In *Putting People First: Sociological Variables in Rural Development*, 2d ed., ed. Michael M. Cernea, 148–87. London: Oxford University Press.

———. 1993. Development-Induced Relocation and Refugee Studies: Thirty-Seven Years of Change and Continuity among Zambia's Gwember Tonga. *Journal of Refugee Studies* 6 (2): 123–52.

———. 1997. Resettlement. In *Water Resources: Environmental Planning, Management, and Development*, ed. Asit K. Biswas, 667–710. New York: McGraw-Hill.

Scudder, Thayer, and Elizabeth Colson. 1972. The Kariba Dam Project: Resettlement and Local Initiative. In *Technology and Social Change*, ed. H. Russell Bernard and Pertti Pelto, 39–69. New York: Macmillan.

———. 1979. Long-Term Research in Gwembe Valley, Zambia. In *Long-Term Field Research in Social Anthropology*, ed. George M. Foster, Thayer Scudder, Elizabeth Colson, and Robert V. Kemper, 227–54. New York: Academic.

———. 1982. From Welfare to Development: A Conceptual Framework for the Analysis of Dislocated People. In *Involuntary Migration and Resettlement: Problems and Responses of Dislocated People*, ed. Art Hansen and Anthony Oliver-Smith, 267–87. Boulder CO: Westview.

Seaver, James E. 1990. *A Narrative of the Life of Mrs. Mary Jemison*. Syracuse NY: Syracuse University Press.

Sharpless, Joshua. 1930 [1798]. A Visit to Cornplanter in 1798: Being Extracts from the Diary of Joshua Sharpless. *Warren (PA) Times Mirror.*

Shkilnyk, Anastasia. 1985. *A Poison Stronger than Love: The De-*

struction of an Ojibwa Community. New Haven: Yale University Press.

Silverman, Martin. 1971. *Disconcerting Issue: Meaning and Struggle in a Resettled Pacific Community.* Chicago: University of Chicago Press.

Simmons, Henry. 1799. Journal of Henry Simmons. MG 220, Box 8. Pennsylvania State Archives, Harrisburg.

Smith, Roland M. 1975, 1977. The Politics of Pittsburgh Flood Control, 1936–1960. *Pennsylvania History* 42 (1): 5–24; 44 (1): 3–24.

Smock, David R. 1969. The Role of Anthropology in a Western Nigerian Resettlement Project. In *The Anthropology of Development in Sub-Saharan Africa,* ed. David Brokensha and Marion Pearsall, 40–47. Society for Applied Anthropology, Monograph no. 10. Lexington: University Press of Kentucky (published for the Society for Applied Anthropology).

Snyder, Peter Z. 1971. The Social Environment of the Urban Indian. In *The American Indian in Urban Society,* ed. Jack O. Waddell and O. Michael Watson, 206–43. Boston: Little, Brown.

Snyderman, George S. 1951. Concepts of Land Ownership among the Iroquois and Their Neighbors. *Bureau of American Ethnology Bulletin* 149 (2): 15–34.

Snyderman, George S., ed. 1957. Halliday Jackson's Journal of a Visit Paid to the Indians of New York (1806). *Proceedings of the American Philosophical Society* 101:565–88.

Sorkin, Alan L. 1978. *The Urban American Indian.* Lexington MA: D. C. Heath.

Spicer, Edward H. 1952a. Resistance to Freedom: Settlement from the Japanese Relocation Centers during World War II. In *Human Problems in Technological Change: A Casebook,* ed. Edward H. Spicer, 245–60. New York: John Wiley and Sons.

Spicer, Edward H., ed. 1952b. *Human Problems in Technological Change: A Casebook.* New York: John Wiley and Sons.

Spring, Anita. 1982. Women and Men as Refugees: Differential Assimilation of Angolan Refugees in Zambia. In *Involuntary Migration and Resettlement: Problems and Responses of Dislocated People,* ed. Art Hansen and Anthony Oliver-Smith, 37–47. Boulder CO: Westview.

Starn, Orin. 1986. Engineering Internment: Anthropologists and the War Relocation Authority. *American Ethnologist* 13:700–720.

Stoffle, Richard W., Cheryl A. Last, and Michael J. Evans. 1979. Reservation-Based Tourism: Implications of Tourist Attitudes for Native American Economic Development. *Human Organization* 38:300–306.

Taswell, Ruth. 1986. Scrap-the-Dam Signature Campaign in Sarawak. *Cultural Survival Quarterly* 10:21.

Thursz, Daniel. 1973. *Where Are They Now? A Study of the Impact of Relocation on Former Residents of Southwest Washington Who Were Served in an HWC Demonstration Project.* Washington DC: Health and Welfare Council of the National Capital Area.

du Toit, Brian M. 1982. Involuntary Migration and Government Policy: Population Displacement in South Africa. In *Involuntary Migration and Resettlement: Problems and Responses of Dislocated People,* ed. Art Hansen and Anthony Oliver-Smith, 139–58. Boulder CO: Westview.

Tome, Philip. 1989 [1854]. *Pioneer Life; or, Thirty Years a Hunter.* Baltimore: Gateway Press.

Tooker, Elisabeth. 1968. On the New Religion of Handsome Lake. *Anthropological Quarterly* 41:187–200.

———. 1978a. Iroquois since 1820. In *Northeast,* ed. Bruce G. Trigger, 449–65. Vol. 15 of *Handbook of North American Indians,* ed. William C. Sturtevant. Washington DC: Smithsonian Institution Press.

———. 1978b. The League of the Iroquois: Its History, Politics, and Ritual. In *Northeast,* ed. Bruce G. Trigger, 418–41. Vol. 15 of *Handbook of North American Indians,* ed. William C. Sturtevant. Washington DC: Smithsonian Institution Press.

———. 1984. Women in Iroquois Society. In *Extending the Rafters: Interdisciplinary Approaches to Iroquoian Studies,* ed. Michael Foster, Jack Campisi, and Marianne Mithun, 109–23. Albany: State University of New York Press.

———. 1995. Personal communication, October, Rensselaerville NY.

Trigger, Bruce G., ed. 1978. *Northeast.* Vol. 15 of *Handbook of North American Indians,* ed. William C. Sturtevant. Washington DC: Smithsonian Institution Press.

U.S. Bureau of Indian Affairs. 1953. Problems of Indian Removal and Rehabilitation Growing out of the Fort Randall Reservoir Taking on the Crow Creek and Lower Brule Reservations, South Dakota. Report no. 136. Billings MT: Missouri River Basin Investigations Project.

U.S. House. 1964. Subcommittee on Indian Affairs of the Committee on Interior and Insular Affairs. *Kinzua Dam (Seneca Indian Relocation): Hearings on H.R. 1794, H.R. 3343, and H.R. 7354.* 88th Cong., 1st sess.

U.S. Senate. 1964. Subcommittee on Indian Affairs of the Committee on Interior and Insular Affairs. *Kinzua Dam (Seneca Indian Relocation): Hearings on S. 1836 and H.R. 1794.* 88th Cong., 2d sess.

Uphoff, Norman. 1991. Fitting Projects to People. In *Putting People First: Sociological Variables in Rural Development,* 2d ed., ed. Michael M. Cernea, 467–511. London: Oxford University Press.

Upton, Helen M. 1980. *The Everett Report in Historical Perspective: The Indians of New York.* Albany: New York State American Revolution Bicentennial Commission.

Valpy, Michael. 1994. After Page 1. *Globe and Mail* (Toronto), 29 January.

Vecsey, Christopher, and William A. Starna, eds. 1988. *Iroquois Land Claims.* Syracuse NY: Syracuse University Press.

Voget, Fred W. 1984. Anthropological Theory and Iroquois Ethnography: 1850 to 1970. In *Extending the Rafters: Interdisciplinary Approaches to Iroquoian Studies,* ed. Michael K. Foster, Jack Campisi, and Marianne Mithun, 343–57. Albany: State University of New York Press.

Waddell, Jack O., and O. Michael Watson, eds. 1971. *The American Indian in Urban Society.* Boston: Little, Brown.

Wadden, Marie. 1996. *Nitassinan: The Innu Struggle to Reclaim Their Homeland.* Vancouver: Douglas & McIntyre.

Wallace, Anthony F. C. 1951. Some Psychological Determinants of Culture Change in an Iroquoian Community. Bureau of American Ethnology *Bulletin* 149 (3): 37–54.

———. 1956a. Revitalization Movements. *American Anthropologist* 58:264–81.

———. 1956b. Tornado in Worcester: An Exploratory Study of Individual and Community Behavior in an Extreme Situation. Publication no. 392. Washington DC: National Academy of Sciences, National Research Council.

———. 1958. The Dekanawideh Myth Analyzed as the Record of a Revitalization Movement. *Ethnohistory* 5:118–30.

———. 1963. Exporting the American Idea: Quaker Technology among the Senecas. *Saturday Review* 46 (14): 54–56.

———. 1967. Revitalization Movements in Development. In *The Challenge of Development: Theory and Practice*, ed. Richard J. Ward, 448–54. Chicago: Aldine.

———. 1969. *The Death and Rebirth of the Seneca.* New York: Vintage.

———. 1978. Origins of the Longhouse Religion. In *Northeast*, ed. Bruce G. Trigger, 442–48. Vol. 15 of *Handbook of North American Indians*, ed. William C. Sturtevant. Washington DC: Smithsonian Institution Press.

———. 1984. The Career of William N. Fenton and the Development of Iroquoian Studies. In *Extending the Rafters: Inter-disciplinary Approaches to Iroquoian Studies*, ed. Michael K. Foster, Jack Campisi, and Marianne Mithun, 1–12. Albany: State University of New York Press.

———. 1993. *The Long, Bitter Trail: Andrew Jackson and the Indians.* New York: Hill and Wang.

Wallace, Anthony F. C., ed. 1952. Halliday Jackson's Journal to the Seneca Indians, 1798–1800. *Pennsylvania History* 19:117–47, 325–49.

Wallace, Paul A. W. 1946. *The White Roots of Peace.* Philadelphia: University of Pennsylvania Press. Reprint, Port Washington NY: I. J. Friedman, 1968.

Wardell, Morris L. 1977. *A Political History of the Cherokee Nation, 1838–1907.* Norman: University of Oklahoma Press.

Washburn, Wilcomb E. 1971. *Red Man's Land/White Man's Law: A Study of the Past and Present Status of the American Indian.* New York: Charles Scribner's Sons.

Washington Post. 1961. Editorial, 8 April.

Wax, Rosalie. 1971. *Doing Fieldwork: Warnings and Advice.* Chicago: University of Chicago Press.

Weinman, Paul L. 1969. *A Bibliography of the Iroquoian Literature:*

Partially Annotated. Bulletin no. 411. Albany: New York State Museum and Science Service.

Weppner, Robert S. 1971. Urban Economic Opportunities: The Example of Denver. In *The American Indian in Urban Society*, ed. Jack O. Waddell and O. Michael Watson, 244–73. Boston: Little, Brown.

White, Leslie A., ed. 1959. *Lewis Henry Morgan: The Indian Journals, 1859–62.* Ann Arbor: University of Michigan Press.

Wilkinson, Charles F. 1987. *American Indians, Time, and the Law: Native Societies in a Modern Constitutional Democracy.* New Haven: Yale University Press.

Wilson, Edmund. 1960. *Apologies to the Iroquois.* New York: Vintage.

World Bank. 1990. Operational Directive 4.30: Involuntary Resettlement. Washington DC: World Bank.

———. 1991. Operational Directive 4.20: Indigenous Peoples. Washington DC: World Bank.

Index